PRODUCTIZE

Praise for *Productize*

"Any leader of a professional services business will recognize the challenge of scaling their business beyond one-time services. *Productize* is a great blueprint for CEOs of B2B professional services firms who are looking to get to the next level of growth by turning IP and services into products that can scale."

– Christoffer Ellehuus, President, KF Digital at Korn Ferry

"Launch BOLDLY! Eisha's wisdom identifies 7 Deadly Productization Mistakes and masterfully offers leaders a simple (yet, not easy) vision & roadmap to sidestep these common mistakes. Eisha goes beyond the productization tools and zeros in on leadership's most challenging role of the *Productize* journey: stonewalling legacy team & an entrenched culture who are complacent with the current business model. Eisha inspires leaders to be bold and fearless."

-Ray Attiyah, Author of The Fearless Frontline

"It is rare to find someone like Eisha who has such extensive experience productizing professional services and teaching other business leaders how to do it themselves. This is not your typical business book where you skim it and wonder why you bought it. *Productize* is a book you can use with your leadership team to study, discuss and use its tools to bring your growth ideas to life."

-Jeff Spanbauer, CEO of Relevate Health Group

"*Productize* is a must-read for leaders of both product and services companies seeking to create scale and growth in their business. It's a great combination of frameworks and sound advice!"

-Simon Frewer, CEO at Challenger

"*Productize* is a must-read for any leader of a services business who wants to scale their organization. It's a powerful playbook for how to create and launch successful products alongside a services business, including relatable case studies and a library of tools for your team to use."

– Jennifer McCollum, CEO at Linkage

"Scaling any business is challenging, even more so for professional services businesses. *Productize* is a handbook for creating successful products that complement existing services, allowing your business to grow revenue without adding costs at the same rate — and without putting your existing business at risk. As Eisha says, 'That's the sweet spot.'"

-Christy Pretzinger, CEO at WriterGirl

"For anyone leading a B2B product initiative — whether building new software or productizing services — this book is a blueprint that will save you time and resources by guiding you around the many pitfalls that you are likely to encounter."

-Dejan Deuzevik, Product Leader

"Product development and roll-out will become the "it capability" in the coming decade as businesses both scale and compete for mind and wallet share from their customers, and as customers, in turn, look for ease of functionality. Armstrong's book is both practical and insightful and provides a clear roadmap for C-level executives."

- Sampriti Ganguli, CEO at Arabella Advisors

PRODUCTIZE

THE ULTIMATE GUIDE TO TURNING PROFESSIONAL SERVICES INTO SCALABLE PRODUCTS

BY

EISHA TIERNEY ARMSTRONG

Productize: The Ultimate Guide to Turning Professional Services into Scalable Products

Published by Vecteris
www.vecteris.com

First Edition

Book Cover Design by ebooklaunch.com

ISBN 978-1-7369296-0-5 (ebook)
ISBN 978-1-7369296-1-2 (paperback)

Printed in the United States of America

THE DEDICATION

To Nicole, for encouraging me to be fearless

Acknowledgments

Thank You!

Eisha and the team at Vecteris want to thank the hundreds of CEOs, executives and Product professionals who have used our services, joined our peer groups or used our tools to support your innovation and growth journeys. You've helped us live our mission to help organizations design and launch forward-thinking products to positively impact the world.

Business Leaders

Several of these leaders and companies are highlighted throughout the book. Thank you for openly sharing your stories and lessons learned so that we might all benefit, specifically: Ray Attiyah, Christopher Ellehuus, David Evans, Simon Frewer, Brian Joseph, Larry Kavanaugh, Christophe Martel, Jennifer McCollum, Anil Prahlad, Christy Pretzinger, Jim Price, Andrew Stockwell, Conrad Schmidt, and Jeff Spanbauer.

Two executives went way beyond the call of duty to review the galley copy and provide critical feedback, which influenced the key teaching points of the book: Dejan Duzevik, entrepreneur and product leader; and Russell Dumas, product leader and cheerleader. Thank you.

The Team

No book gets completed without a talented team of writers, editors, researchers, marketers and designers. Thank you to writing partner Michaela Rawsthorn, who helped extensively with this book and supports the content marketing efforts at Vecteris; Lauri Hershner who helped draw out the insights from the primary research, edited the downloadable tools and provided extensive editing for the book; Perin Goodman for also editing the downloadable tools and keeping us organized; Nicole Merrill for project management and moral support; Gabrielle Blocher and Jaime Drennan for providing support, encouragement and feedback; Matt Stevens and Jon Riley for being our marketing partners; and Olha Yankina for graphic design.

Family and Friends

Thank you to Nicole Ferry and to Sarah Brown for support, encouragement and accountability. And an incredibly large thank you to Eisha's family for their support and patience through the writing of this book, especially during a global pandemic. Thank you to Charlie and Heather for encouraging Eisha to balance writing and play time out in Montana, to David and Calvin for bringing your mom joy and laughter; and to Tim for graciously picking up the slack and for your unwavering belief that Eisha can do anything she sets her mind to.

Contents

Part Three: Be Fearless | 127

Introduction

The Productization Imperative

Investing in Exploration

In 2015, Jim Price set his sights on developing new sources of revenue. Jim is the CEO of Empower, a creative media agency with an annual revenue of around $250 million headquartered in Cincinnati, Ohio. After attending an executive education program on innovation at Northwestern University, Jim decided to invest in innovation with the goal of creating new revenue streams. "I learned," said Jim, "that every business needs both fortifiers, who focus on growing the existing business, and explorers, who focus on creating new revenue streams." Jim created Empower's "Explorer Program" to encourage employees to search the peripheries of Empower's existing business model and identify potential areas of growth.

During the 5-year period, 2015 to 2020, the benefits of this strategy became clear. Jim hired the agency's first Chief Product Officer, and a suite of successful new products was developed that generated recurring revenue. Two of these products include ClearTrade, a programmatic media buying platform, and MediaAgent, a software as a service (SaaS) media planning tool for smaller companies. Empower also utilizes "Brand Labs," an in-house think tank designed to leverage internal marketing capabilities to create Empower's own direct-to-consumer brands. Tanon, a leather goods manufacturer, is one such brand.

Under Jim's leadership, Empower experienced record-breaking revenue growth in 2016, 2017, and 2018. The successful creation of new revenue streams earned prestigious industry titles, including *MediaPost*'s "Media Agency of the Year" and most recently, *Ad Age*'s "Agency A-List Standout," making Empower the first Cincinnati-based agency to receive national recognition. Empower's evolution from a media buying agency to an organization with a portfolio of services and highly scalable products is inspiring; it is also emblematic of the key steps services organizations need to take in order to create scalable products.

Is This Book for You?

Are you considering developing (or perhaps have already begun to develop) products that complement your service business? Either way, you've likely realized that this strategy is difficult to execute well.

Designing, developing, and successfully selling products requires a unique set of skills, business processes, and investments compared to the traditional delivery of services. This book is designed to give you an easy-to-follow blueprint for building new capabilities through the sharing of real-life business examples and practical, results-based tools.

This book will detail ***how to develop and launch successful products*** as opposed to giving advice about which products to create. Consulting company Bain aptly observed that "most leadership teams understand the opportunity for product innovation, but underinvest in the broad changes to the business model and culture that enable speed, learning, and agility."[1] To be successful, our primary focus needs to be: "Do we know how to choose the right innovation investments, test them in real time, and scale them for maximum impact?"[2]

This book was written to fill a gap in the marketplace for professional services organizations (consulting firms, accounting firms, marketing agencies, training companies, etc.) that want to innovate and develop more scalable—often tech-enabled—products. Backed by over twenty years of experience building productized consulting, training, information services, and data services businesses, a great deal of experience shapes my thinking. I've seen many talented leaders make expensive, but easily avoidable, mistakes as they seek to scale and grow using a product strategy. I can help you to avoid making those same mistakes.

After seeing many professional services firms struggle with new product innovation, I co-founded *Vecteris* and began consulting with professional services and other B2B services organizations to help them innovate new products and transition to more recurring revenue business models. As a result of this work, I have cataloged the typical challenges these organizations face in transitioning from services to products. I have also developed and honed a six-part product innovation approach that greatly increases the likelihood of success in this endeavor. This book is built upon that solid framework.

Throughout the book, I've included references to *Vecteris Productization Tools* that help with the implementation of tactics and strategies on the productization journey. For example, prioritization frameworks, the voice of the customer interview guides, a competitor research checklist, sample

1 Baculard, L.P., Colombani, L., Flam, V., Lancry, O. and Spaulding, E. (2017). *Orchestrating a Successful Digital Transformation*. Bain.
2 Ibid.

job descriptions, and much more, are located online. Just look for this icon and go to *www.theproductizebook.com* to download the tools.

What "Product" Means for Business Services Firms

What does it mean for a services organization to *productize*? Let's start by clearly defining a *product*. Product refers to a scalable,[3] often tech-enabled, tool or program that can be packaged and sold. Just like a tube of toothpaste that we might buy at a store, a product has a name, a predefined set of features and benefits, and a set price.

Imagine that you own a marketing consulting firm that utilizes an intelligence database and data analysis methodology to underpin consulting engagements. If that data analysis is only sold in conjunction with highly-customized consulting engagements, your firm's revenue growth will be limited by the speed at which you can add and train staff.

By converting a component of your customized service offering (the database and data analysis methodology) into a product to be sold alongside less scalable customized services (e.g., your consultants' time), your firm could grow its revenue and improve its profit margin. Both the database and data analysis would be offered as a "product" for companies to subscribe to and access through a self-service portal.

This scenario is not hypothetical; on the contrary, it is derived from a real-world example wherein a client attracted new customers by developing a scalable product (thus growing revenue) and then successfully deployed that product (leading to increased profit margins). Neither of these actions put existing consulting services at risk; *that's* the sweet spot.

---

3   *A product is scalable when we can grow revenue at a faster rate than we need to add costs, such as people.*

The Different Flavors of Productization

To really understand what it means to productize services, it helps to understand the different flavors of productization available to services firms. Here is a simple **Innovation Ladder** framework that I developed to map out the various product options:

Innovation Ladder for Services Organizations

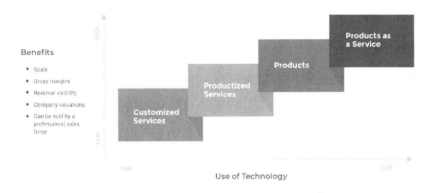

As we move from *Customized Services* in the lower left to *Products as a Service* in the upper right, the use of technology tends to increase (the X-axis) as do the benefits (the Y-axis). Benefits include: improved gross margins, better revenue visibility, and increased company valuation. It is important to note that it's not necessary to move through each phase; however, many companies do follow this progression.

Some organizations use the name "*Technology Enabled Services*" rather than "*Productized Services*" or "*Products,*" or even "*Products as a Service.*" Technology Enabled Services can be an easier concept for staff to understand; that particular label also emphasizes the use of technology to scale.

Progression Along the Innovation Ladder

Many organizations provide **Customized Services** in the form of human-resource intensive, knowledge-led services. This business model is often lucrative, but it's not scalable because it requires additional people to serve additional clients. It's also very "hands-on" and key-person dependent, with the client buying the time and expertise of a consultant/ partner/principal.

The next rung, **Productized Services**, still requires additional people, but it should require fewer resources than Customized Services to both sell and to deliver. Productized services are standardized so that all customers receive the same experience at the same price. The service is broken down into its core components or process steps, which are sold as a defined package. For example, WP Curve (later bought by GoDaddy) productized WordPress consulting by offering a package of website building or website enhancing services. Instead of working one-on-one with a consultant to build or repair a company's website, customers buy the package of services they need (at a fixed price) and the WP Curve team builds or repairs the site on their own. The bundle of services is outlined up front so that the customer knows exactly what they are getting.

The next move up the innovation ladder is to **Products**. Here, features are standardized and packaged for an 'off-the-shelf' buying experience. An example would be a conference with a set agenda designed to attract anyone interested in the specific topic offered. Another example would be a pre-packaged, industry trends report that anyone involved in that particular industry might buy and use.

At the top of the innovation ladder is **Products as a Service.** The customer relationship is ongoing, though the services are still well-defined and standardized. Using the industry trends report example, instead of the customer buying just one report, the customer pays a subscription fee to access a series of reports or supplemental data to complement the reports. The *service* is the ongoing, up-to-date supply of information to the customer, and the *product* is the standardized information itself.

Many services firms are developing subscription-based technology platforms designed to be consumed alongside their traditional consulting services. For example, Accenture's AIP+ service blends traditional consulting with a collection of artificial intelligence (AI) technologies. AIP+ is a cloud-based platform through which Accenture's clients can install AI tools and applications from a network of partner vendors, effectively offering "AI as a service." By partnering with technology vendors, Accenture benefits from being able to offer AI as a service without having to invest in the engineering resources to develop those technologies in-house. Similarly, Accenture's technology partners gain access to new clients and markets without having to sell their services themselves.[4]

I've summarized this information in the table on the next page.

---

4 CB Insights (October 8, 2020). Killing Strategy: The Disruption of Management Consulting.

Offering	Distribution	Delivery	Business Model (Pricing)	Examples
Customized Services	1:1	In-Person or Virtual	Time & Materials, Project or Retainer	Consulting Engagement, Agency Services
Productized Services	1:1	In-Person or Virtual	Transactional, per product pricing, may have different service levels (e.g., silver, gold, platinum)	A service package, pre-defined workshop, or training session
Products	1: Many	In-Person or Virtual	Transactional	Conference, Syndicated Research Report
Products as a Service	1: Many	Virtual	Subscription	Learning as a Service, Data as a Service, Software as a Service, AI as a Service, Membership

Three Ingredients for All Products

Successful **Productized Services**, **Products**, or **Products as a Service** all satisfy a market need through the appropriate combination of:

- Intellectual Property (e.g., content, data, a proprietary process)
- Technology (e.g., application/user interface, tools, analytics)
- Service (e.g., Account Management, Advisor Services, Help Desk)

Intellectual property forms the basis for the product, technology helps it scale, and services help the customer unlock the value. The ratio of each ingredient within the mix is determined by the end goal: are you creating a productized service, a product, or a product as a service? Note the varying ratios of technology, intellectual property, and service for each type of product:

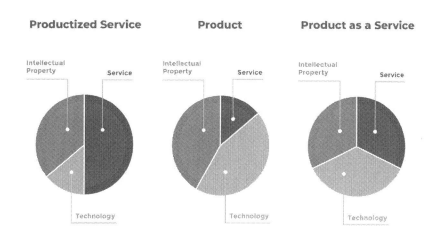

Why You Need a Product Innovation Strategy

Utilizing a product innovation strategy opens up the potential to quickly grow an already large sector of the economy. The global market for professional services firms is approximately $5.7 trillion[5]; traditional consulting services alone accounts for $200 billion of this market.[6] In the decade leading up to COVID-19, these companies enjoyed a compound annual

---

5   *Business Wire (July 1, 2019): The 2019 Global Professional Services Market - Worth $5.7 Billion in 2018; Projected to Surpass $8 Billion by 2022: Research-AndMarkets.com*

6   *CB Insights (October 8, 2020). Killing Strategy: The Disruption Of Management Consulting.*

growth rate (CAGR) of more than 7 percent.[7] So, why should productization be considered an important strategy for professional services firms? Consider the following compelling benefits and drivers:

Scale: Scalable products help to grow revenue at the same rate without having to add costs at the same rate. If I want to increase revenue at my accounting firm, I typically have to add new accountants at the same rate that I add new customers. Even then, my service is only as good as the people delivering it. I have to hire, onboard and train flawlessly so my clients have the same quality experience, no matter who is delivering the service. However, well-designed and delivered products can help grow revenue at two to three times the current rate (if not more) because of the direct and indirect costs associated with hiring, training and ensuring quality across more people.

Better profit margins: A "product" company such as Adobe, Gartner, or Bloomberg typically has gross profit margins ranging from 60 to 90 percent, versus an industry standard of 40 percent for customized professional services.[8] Although there are higher up-front product development investments (more on that in Chapter Four), the introduction of marketable products can increase revenue (scale) with less investment over time.

Improved revenue visibility: Under the influence of COVID-19, the subscription economy has hit a tipping point for both consumer and B2B subscriptions. Subscription payment processor Zuora reported that subscription businesses, on average, are growing revenues 5 times faster than their S&P 500 counterparts (18.2 percent versus 3.6 percent) as

---

7 *Business Wire (July 1, 2019): The 2019 Global Professional Services Market - Worth $5.7 Billion in 2018; Projected to Surpass $8 Billion by 2022: ResearchAndMarkets.com*

8 *Sawhney, M. (2016). Putting Products into Services. Harvard Business Review.*

measured over the last 8 years.[9] Buyers love subscriptions because of the budget visibility and the continuous upgrades (versus quickly becoming obsolete); sellers love subscription-based products because they provide fantastic revenue visibility. One example of a subscription-based product includes a customized training company that developed a learning experience platform that is sold via subscription as a "learning as a service" product. Another example is a marketing consultancy that built a self-serve, marketing intelligence "data as a service" product. The takeaway here is that retainer models can help improve revenue visibility, but they don't have the profit margins associated with "as a service" products.

Higher and easier valuations: Product and "as a service" companies have much higher valuations (e.g., eight times revenue) than traditional professional services firms (e.g., one times revenue) because they have better profit margins and improved revenue visibility.[10] Without distinct products, business service firm valuations are developed using highly subjective variables—such as the defensibility of intellectual property (IP), the strength of relationships with clients, the reliance on founder relationships, and the knowledge and skills of the team.

Accelerating digitization and use of technology: Technology provides the opportunity to deliver services at scale, and especially since COVID-19, many business services customers are willing to receive services virtually. This point was brought home recently when Microsoft CEO Satya Nadella said, "As COVID-19 impacts every aspect of our work and life, we have seen two years' worth of digital transformation in two months."[11] Virtual delivery is typically followed by automated delivery, helping us scale even further.

9   Gold, C. (2019). The Subscription Economy Index. Zuora.

10 Longanecker, C. (2015). Why You Should Use a Subscription Business Model. Entrepreneur.com

11 Spataro, J (2020). 2 years of digital transformation in 2 months. Microsoft.com

Increased competition and disruption: Almost every traditional business services firm that I work with is facing increased competition from digital-first start-ups who are expanding their portfolio by offering services alongside their product. For example, when marketing automation software providers start delivering tailored messaging generated by artificial intelligence technology, they begin to compete with traditional marketing agencies. Consider data analytics software company Palantir, which combines its Palantir Foundry software platform with customized consulting services into a single information product that it licenses to its clients.[12] Once a buyer commits to buying a software product from a vendor, embedding it into existing workflows, and training staff to use it, they are much more likely to purchase add-on services from that same software vendor as opposed to dealing with a services-only company.[13] Software companies have a strong economic incentive to develop more services that they can sell to existing customers.[14]

Simon Frewer, CEO of Challenger, a professional sales training, consulting and technology business, described the environment well: "It's not just an increase of similar kinds of competitors, but a wider array of solutions. There are more options available to B2B buyers than ever before. We aren't just being considered against the top four sales training companies, we are being compared to all of the things that might impact sales and productivity."

CB Insights recently noted how at risk traditional professional services firms are for disruption. Consulting, for example, is still primarily based on hourly billing rather than value-based pricing. Moreover, "the increasing

---

12 *CB Insights (October 8, 2020). Killing Strategy: The Disruption Of Management Consulting.*

13 *Mohajer, S. (2020). Statistics for SaaS Companies + SaaS growth. Blue Tree. com*

14 *Ibid*

pace of technological change means that, more and more, consultants' recommendations are out of date nearly as soon as they're made."[15]

Soren Kaplan, author of *The Invisible Advantage* and a prominent thinker on business strategy and innovation, has pointed out that business services firms with the following attributes are incredibly vulnerable to disruption, especially in a post-COVID-19 world:

- Being highly dependent on human labor to do computational work (since computers can increasingly accomplish those tasks).

- Deriving their value from information asymmetry (i.e., knowing things that clients don't—an edge that is harder to maintain in the Internet age and with the rise of expert networks like Coleman Research).

- Deriving value from armies of "implementers" (since labor and expertise can now be sourced directly by clients using "Human Cloud" services such as freelancer platforms like Upwork. In addition, COVID-19 has effectively removed any on-site advantage; most people are fine with working remotely.)

- Not demonstrating the ability to effectively adapt to digital delivery and being limited to digitally delivering only through video conferencing and collaboration tools. "True differentiation . . . will come from designing offerings based on emerging technologies like no-code software and artificial intelligence to create new digital methodologies that transform clients' fundamental work processes."[16]

---

15 *CB Insights (October 8, 2020). Killing Strategy: The Disruption Of Management Consulting.*

16 *Kaplan, S. (2020). How Consulting Will Likely Change Because of the Pandemic. Inc.com*

- Reliance on one-and-done projects rather than representing a solution that persists (through a subscription) far after the initial engagement ends.[17]

Changes in B2B Buying Behavior: B2C consumers are used to transacting and buying products immediately online and B2B buyers have become accustomed to this as well. This means that professional services organizations have an opportunity to start building relationships with new B2B customers through a simple transaction (a book, an assessment, an online class, a data set) rather than cultivating customers through other marketing and sales techniques. In other words, you can develop a relationship by selling a small product, and then expand the relationship to include larger and more expensive products and 1:1 consulting engagements. Plus, once a customer buys a product, the relationship starts. By implementing the right strategy, building rapport, and providing quality service, these one-off purchases can transition to longer-term, more in-depth service relationships.[18]

Retention of staff: Let's be honest: it can be a slog to trade time or capacity for money and constantly be in selling mode. The traditional professional services model makes it hard to retain the best talent (the sell/deliver/sell/deliver model can be exhausting) and presents challenges in terms of planning for growth.

Reduction of key person dependency: Productization is a critical part of the growth strategy for business services. If our revenue stream depends on a team of experts, then we live or die by the knowledge and skills they bring. As one CEO confided in me, "Our expertise was all housed in

---

17 Ibid

18 PrWeb (April 2, 2020). A new way to do business online: Major Tom demonstrates the way companies need to evolve in a post-COVID-19 world.

human capital. Any single consultant, or facilitator, or coach—all were operating based on their own expertise. This model is incredibly hard to scale and grow without buying one more human at a time."

I hope this list makes a strong case for a product strategy, especially in the wake of COVID-19. If the pandemic has shown us anything, it's that organizations need to be nimble and willing to change in order to meet the evolving needs of clients and customers. Firms have moved to digital delivery at breakneck speeds, but what they are learning—and many organizations already know—is that digitization and productization aren't just smart ways to ride out a crisis. As was noted in a recent McKinsey article, "During the current crisis, businesses have worked faster and better than they dreamed possible just a few months ago. Maintaining that sense of possibility will be an enduring source of competitive advantage."[19]

Action Steps

1. Plot your current products and services along the Innovation Ladder. Next, plot the new product and service ideas that you are considering. Which ideas have the most compelling benefits? How can you use technology to improve the benefits?

2. What are the reasons behind your pursuit of productization? Are you driven by competitive threats? If so, what kinds of threats are you facing? Perhaps you see productization as a way to open up opportunities . . . If so, which benefits are most important to you, your shareholders, and your employees?

---

19 Sneader, K. and Sternfels, B. (May 1, 2020). From surviving to thriving: Reimagining the post-COVID-19 return. McKinsey.

Chapter One

Seven Deadly Productization Mistakes

Although having a productization strategy is more important than ever for growth and competitiveness, it is difficult to execute well. Product failure rates are estimated to be somewhere between 40 percent[20] and 70 percent.[21] And while 72 percent of executives feel competitive pressure to build and launch technology-enabled, data-driven products, research has found that only about a third of these digital products will succeed.[22]

Why?

As I mentioned before, moving from services to products requires a unique set of skills, business processes, and investments than most service firms typically possess. For companies that deliver highly customized services, new product development and commercialization are often outside of their

20 Castellion, George, and Stephen K. Markham. "Perspective: New Product Failure Rates: Influence of Argumentum ad Populum and Self-Interest." Journal of Product Innovation Management 30, no. 5 (2013): 976-979.

21 Ramanujam, Madhavan, and Georg Tacke. Monetizing Innovation. 2016

22 CapGemini Consulting and MIT Sloan Management (2011). Digital Transformation: A Roadmap for Billion-dollar Organizations.

core skills, processes and mindsets. Productizing services typically requires organizations to think differently about how they work and how they create value for their customers—and this change does not come easily.

There are seven key mistakes that organizations often make. I call them the Seven Deadly Productization Mistakes:

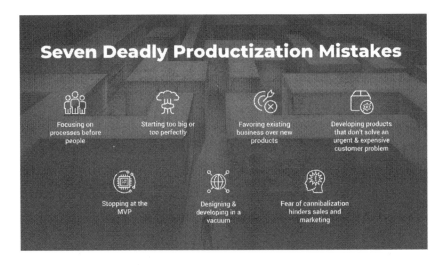

Thankfully, there are ways to avoid each mistake and most companies can implement them easily.

Mistake No. 1

Focusing on Processes Before People

Services businesses that fail to develop successful new products typically don't fail due to a lack of vision. And it's not that the team isn't creative or smart. Often, failure results because of the human factor: people tend to favor the routine, the known, and the comfortable. Productizing services takes most of us outside our comfort zones and into uncharted territory. A productization strategy almost always requires new skills, significant behavior change, and new organizational structures.

Transitioning from customized services to more scalable products can be a significant shift for an organization. Rather than creating tailored solutions for each client (customized services), we move to the phase of creating products that meet 80 percent of the needs of a sizable market segment (scalable products). This shift from one-to-one to one-to-many can be very uncomfortable for people who have distinguished their careers by delighting and catering to individual clients. Making this shift is also likely outside of their core skills. Moreover, investing in a few key "product hires" will not support such radical change.

In order to successfully make the transition, it's important to create a Product-Friendly Culture that focuses on people, not the new product development process. Creating a Product-Friendly Culture includes:

- The CEO and leadership team first articulating a **clear vision** for the product strategy, such as: "In the next three years we are going to impact one hundred more companies, while only growing costs at half the rate."

- The leadership team needs to start **modeling new behaviors**, such as embracing a rapid test-and-learn approach to new product development or sacrificing short-term client revenue for longer-term product revenue.

- The leadership team will also need to develop **new skills,** such as increasing their technical acumen and investing in new skills such as UI/UX design, engineering, analytics, product management, product marketing, and a different sales approach.

- With all of these new skills and behaviors will come the challenge of **managing a much more diverse organization.** Organizational norms and behaviors will need to be developed in order to successfully integrate and leverage a new range of skills, thoughts, and experiences.

- Finally, an **organizational structure** that facilitates collaboration and agility must be developed.

Mistake No. 2

Starting Too Big or Too Perfectly

Many organizations lose money on new product development and/or get lapped by competitors because they take too long to build and launch a product. Worse still, they invest too much in a product with a poor market fit. These organizations often use long, waterfall development processes with "stage gates" to advance to the next level of investment. It can take many months, if not years, before any real market feedback on their ideas is gleaned.

Successful product innovators adopt a rapid, experimental approach to product development. This is also referred to as an MVP or Minimum Viable Product approach. The MVP concept comes from *The Lean Startup* by Eric Ries, which posits that traditional, linear waterfall development or R&D stage gates should be replaced by iterative, agile techniques. Ries saw similarities between the more agile, iterative way of operating and the Toyota Production System, which had become known as Lean Manufacturing. Hence the name "Lean Startup."[23]

An MVP is defined as "the smallest experiment that either proves or disproves [our] assumptions about a business idea."[24] Ries calls it a "build, measure, learn loop."

- "Build" a product we think customers want

- "Measure" if and how they use it

- "Learn" from what customers do and say about the product

- "Loop" back to the beginning to build again

This system allows us to test our products in real life with real buyers and users in order to validate a product's core value. MVP tests are designed to answer technical questions about the product, prove or disprove hypotheses, and get a real feel for the viability of the product in the market. MVPs help avoid costly mistakes.

The point is that our products do not have to be perfect to go to market. They should be good, but *they don't have to be flawless.*

Sal Khan of Khan Academy, a vanguard innovator in online learning, said it best: "shipping is better than perfection." At Khan, the team prioritizes getting their online courses launched on their site over releasing the most perfect version of the courses. Khan delivers a useful course that is

23 Blank, Steve. May 2013. "Why the Lean Startup Changes Everything." Harvard Business Review.

24 Jerry Cao quoted in: Shevchenko, O. (2018). MVP vs MDP = Viability vs Delight. What You Really Need? Medium.com

well-functioning, but with plenty of room for improvement. Instructors and developers listen to what their users tell them about their experience with the course. That way future iterations deliver a product that is closer to what their users want and need.

To best communicate this point to executives, I love requoting Reid Hoffman, the founder of LinkedIn: "If you are not embarrassed by the first version of your product, you've launched too late."

This quote is so important because the best way to test an innovation is to see if the market will buy or use it. This idea may be anxiety-inducing for those with perfectionist tendencies. Launching quickly but imperfectly requires reframing our thinking to include the notion that we are building something good in order to (eventually) make it great.

Mistake No. 3

Favoring Existing Business Over New Products

West Point graduate, leadership consultant, and author Jack McGuinness defines *alignment* as occurring when "all members of the team work in sync to accomplish a common purpose. More specifically, an aligned leadership team debates well, proactively supports each other, is laser focused on what is most important, and is committed to learning and improving."[25] Alignment is an incredibly important component of a successful product innovation strategy. A lack of alignment between share-holders on the investment required to build and launch new products is a recipe for underinvestment. Additionally, a lack of alignment between

---

25 McGuinness, J. (August 31, 2018). Alignment is the Cornerstone of Great Leadership Teams. Chief Executive Group, LLC.

organizational leaders on the strategies and performance measures will doom product receptivity well before launch.

To meaningfully grow more scalable revenue streams, organizations need to make investments. Many business services firms begin new product development by selling new products as part of client engagements (i.e., the new product is not developed until one client agrees to pay for it). It's also common practice to assign new product development as a "special project" to client-facing staff to be worked on after hours, or when existing work is slow. While this may work for the first six to twelve months, this half-hearted arrangement doesn't lead to a viable, long-term resourcing strategy.

Executives often believe that existing consulting/account management/sales teams can begin selling newly-developed products, and that consultants and analysts can take on the management of product development. In reality, the shift requires fresh talent in the organization, which requires up-front investment.

New product development done "off the side of the desk" of existing staff is rarely successful because client demands (and immediate revenue) are always a higher priority. One Chief Product Officer of an organization undergoing this shift remarked: "We always prioritize the client's concern. In the moment of tough tradeoffs, it's very hard to say no to a client to go build a product."

Organizations fail when they do not devote initial resources to new product development. Allocating staff time for a design sprint, and a dedicated budget for fast-cycle market research or concept development are examples of a few worthwhile up-front investments.

Importantly, it's not just seed investment that is required. Similar to the venture capital corollary, organizations need to set aside funds to make appropriate additional product investments once an idea starts to gain traction (i.e., "investment powder"). As Simpact CEO and Co-Founder Dejan Duzevik shared, it's difficult to transition to productization by bootstrapping or taking a piecemeal approach by building a feature here and there. "To be successful," he says, "we must fully commit and invest."

And this brings us back to alignment. Allocating sufficient resources to fund both product development and product launch typically requires changing shareholder expectations. Using a $20 million firm as an example, the research, ideation, and concept testing stages typically cost at least 1 to 2 percent of revenue; full concept development and launch can cost 5 to 20 percent of revenue. These investments need not be made all at once, but at some point, they will need to be made.

As with any investment portfolio, allocation and alignment decisions need to be made with regard to how much to invest, as well as how the product development portfolio will be managed across product types. How much capital should be invested in moonshot ideas versus easy, product line extensions?

Many new business ventures and products fail because organizations attempt to use existing metrics and processes to assess and manage new products. This lack of flexibility often spells failure for new product launches because of the immediate, negative consequences. New products that ultimately fail to "compete" for focus and funding generate less revenue, lower profit margins, and use more resources as they go through the launch process (as compared to existing products and services). This is a big area of concern.

The simple truth is this: a focus on the current year's output and revenue will never spur on innovation; a company may run successfully for a while on this mindset, but it will be hard to remain competitive. For example, one consulting organization quickly realized that their emphasis on measuring billable hours was creating a disincentive for staff to sell and service products that were not sold on a billable hours basis.

Successful organizations develop innovation-friendly metrics, such as:

- The number of new, viable product ideas generated per year
- The ability to launch new, road mapped products on schedule
- The number of new customers gained since product launch
- Overall product revenue and profitability

Mistake No. 4

Not Solving an Urgent and Expensive Problem

A major mistake I see companies make is developing a new product that does not solve an urgent and expensive problem that customers are experiencing. The error can happen when an organization falls in love with new technology and jumps to develop a product that uses the technology. And it can happen when a company fixates on leveraging existing intellectual property they've already developed, forgetting to ask if customers really need or want it. In both of these cases, companies are developing a "solution in search of a problem."

Sometimes a product team thinks they've identified an urgent and expensive customer problem, but it's really only a *frequently cited* problem. For example, my team recently completed a new product development project for a client whose business was placing professionals in out-of-town assignments. We started the project with a series of Voice of the Customer interviews. Many of the professionals we interviewed talked about the loneliness they felt while on out-of-town work assignments. In digging deeper, we realized that the problem of loneliness was not as painful as other problems, such as job assignment uncertainty, or access to better temporary housing options. Loneliness was a *frequently cited* problem, but not an *urgent and expensive* problem. We recommended to our client that they focus innovation efforts on solving the problems of job assignment uncertainty and better temporary housing options and think about addressing loneliness at a later date.

Sometimes an organization identifies an urgent and expensive problem, but it's in relation to a market segment that is too small, too price-sensitive, and/or is not a good fit with their core services. For example, one copywriting services company decided to use their existing internal writing training program for new employees and develop it into a new product that clients could buy to train their own staff. Unfortunately, after spending more than $100,000 developing the new external-facing program, they found that the only companies interested in the training were the small handful of very large companies with teams of in-house copywriters. The Total Addressable Market (TAM)[26] for this product was too small.

Other times, one customer's request may be mistaken as representative of the needs of many customers. For example, the client of a training and development company asked for virtual delivery of a 9 class training series to help reduce travel costs (this was pre-COVID-19). Without validating whether other clients had the same need, the company spent well into 6 figures building an online platform that only one company actually wanted.

---

26 *The Total Addressable Market is the overall revenue opportunity if 100% market share is achieved. Revenue opportunity is calculated by knowing the number of customers in the market and the average price point.*

In each of these cases, money was wasted developing and launching new products that did not have a market.

Mistake No. 5

Designing and Developing in a Vacuum

Heidi Grant Halvorson's book, *Reinforcements: How to Get People to Help You* explores the reasons why people hate to ask for help. One common reason is to avoid the perception of not having the answer. This happens frequently during new product innovation. Even when taking the time to conduct upfront market research to identify customers' urgent and expensive problems, many organizations still design and develop in isolation; potential buyers or users don't see the product until it is beautifully finished. Products developed in this way typically fail.

The most successful companies take a co-creation approach to both design and development. Co-creation means involving people outside of the product team in the development and ideation of a product. This includes ideating with employees outside of the core team, as well as with customers and developers.

The concept of new product co-creation was developed in 2003 by C.K. Prahalad and Venkat Ramaswamy,[27] but the concept really took off when LEGO started using it to develop new kits. Anyone can submit an idea to LEGO for a new product, and the product is voted on by other platform users. If the idea is popular enough, the company will develop it and share 1 percent of the profits with the idea's originator.

---

27 Prahalad, C. K., & Ramaswamy, V. (2004). Co-creation experiences: The next practice in value creation. Journal of interactive marketing, 18(3), 5-14.

UK-based Lloyds Banking Group is a good example of successful innovation based on involving multiple stakeholders. In 2006, Lloyds was struggling to keep up with fintech start-ups; their processes were slow and innovation wasn't happening at the required speed. Co-led by a senior IT executive and a senior business executive, they created a digital services unit to begin their digital transformation. The co-leadership aspect helps to ensure that digital innovations are developed with both technology and operations in mind. "Not only does the unit deliver the technology solutions for the bank's new digital retail banking initiatives, but it also ensures that business processes are adapted appropriately," reports Capgemini Consulting.[28] Today, Lloyds is the UK's largest digital bank.

Mistake No. 6

Starving Products Due to Fear of Cannibalization of Higher-Priced Services

Another obstacle to good product innovation is the tendency for an organization to protect what they have. Many organizations run away from products that they fear might cannibalize revenue from existing, often higher-priced services.

However, if we don't risk disrupting our own services and products, someone else will. The faster pace of global change—enabled by technology and increased access to capital—has substantially increased the number of competitors for most companies, especially the digitally disruptive competitors. However, protectionism can lead to obsolescence.

---

28 Capgemini Consulting (2014). The Digital Transformation Symphony: When IT and Business Play in Sync.

For example, one market research firm realized that 60 percent of the custom analysis they were doing for clients could be automated because it consisted of simple data capture and reporting. They explored the possibility of creating a self-serve reporting dashboard for clients to use to access this data, rather than having staff generate reports. The Chief Product Officer shared that, "The idea of automating the reporting and giving our customers self-serve access to it terrifies most of the business leaders because it represents sixty percent of the work that we do now for clients. However, if we don't do it, someone else will."

Businesses willing to cannibalize their existing revenue streams are more likely to survive. Many executives get caught up in the fear that more scalable (often less expensive) products will detract from, or destroy, their existing business. In truth, new products cannibalizing our existing business is the best-case scenario. Sooner or later, competitors will erode our revenue if we aren't willing to risk business as usual.

Consider this advice from Scott Anthony, co-author of *Dual Transformation: How to Reposition Today's Business While Creating the Future*: ". . . companies must come to grips with their cannibalization concerns because getting overly defensive can curtail powerful growth strategies." Or, in the words of Steve Jobs: "If you don't cannibalize yourself, someone else will."

The best advice is to abandon the idea of totally protecting existing services. Instead, think about how new products could attract new customers and eventually drive them to the existing services, or how new products might complement existing services. Mapping how customers may go from products to services and back to products is an important part of this work.

Mistake No. 7

Stopping at the MVP

MVP "learning loops" are only helpful if we commit to continuing to develop and evolve our product after we've launched it. This is hard for organizations with a history of long R&D cycles, or those not used to staffing post-launch teams to make a product better. We need the capacity to measure what we have learned from the MVP launch, develop new hypotheses about the next stage of growth, and use reserve investment dollars and people to improve the product.

Take Dyson vacuums, for example. Dyson Ltd. is a billion-dollar company whose leading product took 5,271 prototypes to create.[29] The inventor, James Dyson, learned something new from every version he created, thereby improving the product with each successive iteration. This test-and-learn philosophy is still used by the more than 3,000 engineers employed at Dyson today. It's safe to assume that these engineers don't need as many prototypes as their founder did; they leverage a global market of users who feed information about what's working and what's not through their buying decisions.

The MVP is only valuable when we make changes based on what we learn. That means we need to accept that the first version will include mistakes. The important part of this trade-off involves listening to customers when they point out those mistakes, and then fixing them in the next product iteration. The MVP is built on the best information available at the time, but it's not going to be perfect because that information is incomplete. This quote from Christopher Moisan, Product Principal at the global design firm Idean, sums it up well: "We still have our known-knowns to build

29 *Patel, S. (2015). 8 Successful Products That Only Exist Because of Failure. Forbes.*

and deliver on and there's the unknown-unknowns—things that crop up during our product development journey that we need to address."[30] The MVP helps to uncover the "unknown-unknowns" in order to improve the product and in the long run, delight more customers.

The Good News

Fortunately, there is a blueprint for how to avoid each of these missteps. We'll explore it more in the next chapter, but it follows three simple principles:

- Think Big, Start Small
- Follow Urgent, Expensive Customer Problems
- Be Fearless

Action Steps

1. Review the seven mistakes and ask yourself: *How likely is it that my organization will fall victim to each one?*

2. List areas of strength (i.e., least susceptibility) and weakness (i.e., greatest susceptibility).

---

30 Maison, C. (May 30, 2019). *Why you need to stop obsessing about our MVP.* Medium.com

PART ONE

THINK BIG, START SMALL

The Productize Pathway

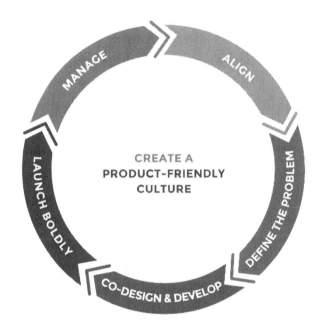

MANAGE

ALIGN

LAUNCH BOLDLY

DEFINE THE PROBLEM

CO-DESIGN & DEVELOP

CREATE A
PRODUCT-FRIENDLY
CULTURE

Chapter Two

MISTAKE: Starting Too Big or Too Perfectly
SOLUTION: The Productize Pathway

The nature of a product and its role in a company's value proposition are not the same for a services firm when compared to a manufacturing firm. The Productization Pathway also will help organizations avoid the Seven Deadly Productization Mistakes. firm. Many of the challenges, especially those around skills and behaviors, alignment, and cannibalization fears, are unique to a services firm. This means that services firms must take a unique approach when designing, developing, and monetizing products.

I have developed a product innovation method uniquely designed to help business services organizations avoid the *Seven Deadly Productization Mistakes* we just explored. I call this method the Productize Pathway™.

This method is designed to help business services organizations boost the speed of product innovation efforts, increase customer focus, and evolve their culture to be more product-friendly.

To start, rather than creating a "set in stone" strategy, a set of hypotheses is created that is continually tested through market experiments. As I mentioned earlier, this approach is deliberately structured as a build, measure, learn loop (hence the circular structure). Building off of *Lean Startup* principles, this is an iterative journey. An iterative process allows us to *Think Big, Start Small.* We run small experiment after small experiment to gradually help us climb the ladder to define and launch our larger product vision.

This process also borrows from Design Thinking methods, which makes it very customer-centric. According to industry leader IDEO, "Design Thinking is a human-centered approach to innovation—anchored in understanding customer's needs, rapid prototyping, and generating creative ideas—that will transform the way you develop products, services, processes, and organizations."[31]

As I'll explain in more depth in the following chapters, each step of the Productize Pathway includes its own discovery loop where we are constantly learning and making changes to our product based on what we've learned—all of which is rooted in our understanding of our customer.

The rest of this book is structured around the Productize Pathway. Let's start in the center of the circle with the fundamentals of **Creating a Product-Friendly Culture**. This is where we win employees' hearts and minds and gradually change behavior across the entire organization; we bring in new skills and learn how to effectively manage and leverage more diversity, and we develop more collaborative and cross-functional ways of working.

Now let's move to **Align** at the top of the circle. Here, we set aside sufficient resources to fund product development, determine how to allocate these resources across a portfolio of product options, and separate the operational metrics and processes used to run the existing business from those used to launch and scale new services. We set a regular tempo of

31 IDEO. Design Thinking. https://www.ideou.com/pages/design-thinking

engaging stakeholders with updates about product development and performance and discussing new investments.

Next, **Define the Problem**. The goal in this stage is to understand the urgent and expensive problems found in the most attractive market segments. This is part *stellar customer listening*, part *data analysis*, and part *strong associative thinking* to spot patterns that no one else can see. This includes:

- Understanding customers' urgent and expensive problems
- Knowing how these problems present by different segments or personas
- Understanding the competitive landscape

Co-Design and Develop come next. This is where we generate, test, and develop ideas. This co-creation model involves ideating with employees outside of the core team, heavily engaging potential with customers, and closely partnering with developers. This includes:

- Developing and cataloging new ideas
- Developing preliminary business models and modeling the revenue and profit potential
- Quickly testing concepts with customers and prospects
- Translating market requirements into product requirements that designers and developers can use to develop an MVP
- Working with designers to build and test prototypes
- Working closely with developers to build a functioning front and back-end
- Continuously soliciting user feedback

As we are developing, we are also planning to Launch Boldly. Here, we think about how new products will attract new customers and eventually lead them to consume existing, yet complementary, services.

This phase includes:

- Developing pricing strategies and packages to target different segments

- Creating messaging to articulate the value proposition

- Creating a multi-channel marketing plan

- Creating a sales strategy and winning the hearts and minds of the sales team

Finally, we move into **Manage & Iterate**. This is where we learn from the market and begin to iterate and repeat an abbreviated version of this cycle again to improve and grow our product. This includes having:

- A customer onboarding process and a usage measurement process to ensure customers are using the product they purchased

- Regular product performance reviews and roadmap updates

- Regular discussion on how the overall portfolio of products is performing

From making the decision to invest in a product strategy to measuring and iterating on that strategy, this book will provide tools, templates, and stories of how other business services firms have used this process to successfully develop, launch, and grow new products. This will help you get where you need to go with confidence and speed. But as you read through this book, keep in mind that each part of the framework can be implemented over time and in small increments (remember: *Think Big, Start Small*).

Before diving in, I highly recommend determining your organization's product innovation maturity by taking a quick assessment at: *www. vecteris.com/diagnostic*. This proprietary Product Innovation Maturity Diagnostic will help you better understand the strengths and weaknesses of your team's current product innovation capabilities. Revisit the assessment as often as you like to track the progress and identify new areas of focus.

The Productize Pathway also will help organizations avoid the Seven Deadly Productization Mistakes.

Productization Mistakes	Solution
Focusing on Processes Before People	Create a Product-Friendly Culture
Starting Too Big or Too Perfectly	Use the Productization Pathway
Favoring Existing Business Rather Than New Products	Align to Support Innovation
Developing Products that Don't Solve an Urgent and Expensive Customer Problem	Define the (Right) Problem
Designing and Developing in a Vacuum	Co-Design and Develop
Starving Products Due to Fear of Cannibalization of Higher Priced Services	Launch Boldly
Stopping at the MVP	Manage and Iterate

Whatever your product innovation maturity, it's my hope that this book gives you the knowledge, tools, and support you need to turn customized services quickly and successfully into scalable products.

Action Steps

1. Assess your organization's product innovation capabilities by taking the Product Innovation Maturity Diagnostic at: *www.vecteris.com/diagnostic*.

2. Revisit the assessment as often as you like to track your progress and identify new areas of focus.

The Productize Pathway

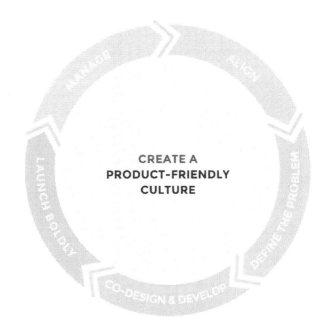

CREATE A
PRODUCT-FRIENDLY
CULTURE

ALIGN

DEFINE THE PROBLEM

CO-DESIGN & DEVELOP

LAUNCH BOLDLY

MANAGE

Chapter Three

MISTAKE: Focusing on Processes Before People
SOLUTION: Create a Product-Friendly Culture

Creating a product-friendly culture is central to building successful products; that's why it's represented in the center of the Productize Pathway. You've probably heard the adage about the three most important things in real estate: "location, location, location." Something similar can be said for innovating a shift from services to products where it's all about "people, people, people." During the shift, we need to bring our whole organization along (which I will explain more in detail throughout this chapter), but I want to be clear that we also need people who are dedicated solely to product innovation. Furthermore, we must provide them with sufficient resources for test-and-learn development. I can't emphasize this enough: *it is hard to innovate and operate at the same time.* Most teams are already spending forty plus hours each week just doing their jobs, and the reality is that existing client work will always take priority. There is usually little, if any, time to think about much else. So, it's critical to prioritize creativity and innovation, even if you are only able to allocate one person to this endeavor.

Now back to the organizational change that focuses on people over process. As I mentioned in Chapter One, I've seen companies fail because they didn't have a clear and inspiring vision, the right behaviors, the right skills, and the right organizational structure. These companies had strong potential to create good products, but the necessary framework wasn't in place. Designing an organization that allows scalable products to thrive doesn't happen overnight. Consider this:

When we move ...

From ...	... To
1:1	1:Many
Selling time and expertise	Selling (often tech-enabled) intellectual property

Our behavior and culture needs to shift ...

From ...	... To
Know	Discover
Scarcity Thinking	An abundance mindset
Perfection	Speed
Individual heroics	Cross-functional collaboration

Making these changes to our culture and way of operating is a significant challenge, but without them, the best products will fail. These changes take commitment and talented change management. And they depend on a few core principles:

- A strong, well-articulated vision
- Behavior change from the top down
- Hiring or developing the right skills
- Diversity of experience and thought

- An organizational structure that facilitates collaboration and agility

- Company-wide technical acumen

- A test-and-learn mindset

A Strong, Well-articulated Vision and Behavior Change

Jeff Spanbauer is CEO of Relevate Marketing, a healthcare marketing agency. He is guiding the organization through a multi-year shift away from highly customized projects to more standardized solutions for their healthcare clients. To be successful, Jeff had to start with a clear vision. As he told me, "Change is always ten times harder than you expect. Without a clear vision for the strategy change, people won't change their behavior."

Jeff also shared that even with a strong vision, behavior change is difficult if a business is doing well. COVID-19 has been a great accelerator in many spheres; Jeff encourages leaders to take advantage of the disruptive changes in the market, or in customer behavior. "If our clients can move from taking six months to shoot a commercial to taking three days, and I can get my entire organization moved onto Microsoft Teams in one week, then we can also make the other changes we need to accelerate our product strategy."

Another great example of the importance of vision and behavior change comes from Jennifer McCollum and Linkage. When Jennifer joined Linkage, Inc. as CEO in 2018, she began to look for ways to scale the company's services. Linkage is a leadership development consultancy that specializes in assessing, training, and coaching leaders. The organization has been in business for more than thirty years. While the company had evolved over time, it still relied on a people-intensive, highly-customized services model. So, Jennifer began to develop a productization strategy that has transformed the way Linkage works and generates revenue.

Change didn't come easily, but Jennifer's success was built upon a strong, well-articulated vision and the desire to change behaviors from the top down. In addition to investing in new technology and talent, productizing Linkage's services required a complete cultural makeover. Jennifer started by anchoring the process around the ambitious vision of impacting leadership effectiveness and equity in 500 organizations by 2022; however, meeting this goal would require Linkage to step away from providing highly-customized services. But vision alone was not enough, and in response to this, Jennifer stated, "We knew that if we didn't address the cultural challenge, we weren't going to achieve our aspirations."

She developed a framework to change company culture one behavior at a time. Based on the book *Culture by Design* by David Friedman, Jennifer developed The Linkage Way, which focuses on cultivating behaviors representative of the organization's values, as well as creating a favorable environment for transitioning from customized services to more scalable solutions. Jennifer made a list of twenty desirable behaviors for everyone in the organization to work toward adopting; each behavior reflected Linkage's new, product-minded personality. The behaviors include qualities such as, "I ask questions and I bring ideas," "I adopt new technology," and "I seek out multiple perspectives."

Jennifer realized that it wasn't enough just to tell people about these behaviors—she also had to ensure that staff adopted them. Moreover, that process had to start with her and the leadership team. On a weekly basis and beginning with Jennifer, one member of the leadership team shared his or her experiences to do with witnessing or practicing one of the organizational behaviors. Linkage leaders began communicating and reinforcing these behaviors in town halls and weekly meetings in order to provide continuous reminders and examples of the behaviors in action, and for everyone to see them being celebrated. The targeted ways of thinking and acting were also integrated into the performance management process. Now, the practice of sharing experiences has been rolled out company-wide. Employees from all divisions and at all levels discuss their experiences with The Linkage Way organizational behaviors on the internal chat board. The new philosophy has seeped into the very fabric of Linkage, helping bring about the change needed to achieve Linkage's goal.

It's important to note that the vision Jennifer created—impacting leadership effectiveness and equity in 500 organizations by 2022—required the organization to adopt a *product* strategy along with a new culture. Linkage did not have the capacity to provide 500 organizations with highly customized services, but with a product strategy, they could create the capacity to serve 500 organizations. Jennifer's vision also focused on increasing the number of clients impacted, as opposed to just thinking about revenue. Organizations often create strategic visions, such as: "By 2022, 25 percent of revenue will come from scalable products." While these visions definitely drive focus around creating and growing scalable products, they don't engage employees' hearts as much as a vision that is tied to increasing the number of clients they can positively serve.

The behaviors that Jennifer outlined for the Linkage team were an important adjunct to her vision. My short list of the top three behaviors for organizations to focus on in their journey to developing scalable products would be:

- Asking questions and bringing ideas
- Practicing blameless problem solving
- Staying open to change

Hiring or Developing the Right Skills

Beyond articulating a clear and compelling vision and encouraging the right behaviors, Jennifer had to work through many layers of challenges, such as executive team buy-in and bringing in new skills. Like Linkage, many organizations find on this journey that although they may have highly talented Subject Matter Experts (SMEs) and successful client relationship builders, they don't have people with product management and technology skills. That often means they need to hire qualified staff or develop the needed skills.

Jeff Spanbauer of Relevate found that he had to bring in outside talent with product experience. "Product people have technical skills that we did not have in-house, but they also think differently. To change our organizational mindset away from customized services to scalable products, we needed outside help," said Jeff. "We made new hires, but we also worked with outside consultants and trainers to teach us product skills."

What do we mean by "product" skills? These competencies include being able to:

- Identify breakthrough product opportunities based on data and pattern spotting (strategy/vision)

- Translate those breakthroughs into a great user experience (design) and financial plans (business)

- Guide product functionality (development)

- Define how the product shows up in the market and gains successful sales (marketing and commercial acumen)

- Analyze product usage data (analytics)

- Ensure that customers, prospects, and staff are aware of, trained on, and engaged with the changing product (management)

Soft skills such as communication, cross-functional influence, the ability to problem solve, and strong execution skills are equally important. People who can work with uncertainty and doubt are also needed. Cleverly labeled as "Chaos Pilots," these are people who can "create structure within chaos and take action."[32]

Leaders of organizations often attempt to turn an existing SME or great relationship builder into a Product Manager or the Head of Product, rather than bringing in an external hire who has product management experience: this is a mistake. Just because someone has strong subject matter expertise or customer knowledge doesn't mean that she or he will be a great product leader. As the adage goes, don't try to put a square peg into a round hole.

It may be tempting to make your Head of Consulting or Client Services your new Head of Product. Before doing that, however, you need to look back at the productization competency list. Ask yourself, how many of the competencies does she have? If the answer is *only those around client knowledge and revenue generation,* then she will fail because she will have a difficult time designing products that meet the needs of a large market segment (versus just the needs of one client). A Product Leader needs user experience, business model strategies, and analytics skills.

It's also a mistake to put someone in a Product Leader role who has strong technical capabilities, but who is weaker in the areas of interpersonal skills and commercial acumen. A person with this profile often struggles to support sales, and they lack the varied skill set necessary to get work done across the enterprise.

---

32 Pisano, G. (2019). *The Hard Truth About Innovative Cultures. Harvard Business Review: Boston.*

COMPETENCIES OF GOOD PRODUCT MANAGERS

SAMPLE PRODUCT MANAGEMENT JOB DESCRIPTIONS
(Visit *www.theproductizebook.com* to download the tools.)

Diversity of Experience and Thought

When bringing in people with productization skills, it's important that the new hires don't become "organ rejection" victims of a company not used to assimilating people with a product skill set. I've worked with clients who have spent hundreds of thousands of dollars to recruit, hire, and train product leaders and developers only to have them fail because at best, the existing team members couldn't understand how to communicate with the new staff and at worst, felt threatened and therefore actively tried to undermine the new hires. In order to stave off these undesired outcomes, it's important to commit to welcoming and leveraging the diversity of experience and thought when bringing in those who possess sought-after skills.

I've been incredibly lucky to have a firsthand view of exceptional product innovation borne of great diversity. My most successful product teams have also been the most diverse in terms of gender, ethnicity, age, and sexual orientation, not to mention cognitive thinking styles and socio-economic backgrounds. Yet, they have developed incredibly innovative products that far exceeded our profit targets. Experience has shown this much to be true: diversity of all kinds leads to better products.

If your organization has historically put a premium on cultural fit and referrals when hiring, you will likely struggle with successfully bringing in diverse talent and building a more inclusive organization. Invest in training leaders who can help your staff to practice inclusive behaviors, including how to create "psychological safety" on teams. Leaders create psychological safety by welcoming diverse ideas and trying out new suggestions. They can also use failure as a teachable moment for all by avoiding blame and choosing to harvest lessons about what worked and what didn't.[33] Acquiring outside help to teach your leaders these inclusivity skills is strongly suggested.

An Organizational Structure that Facilitates Collaboration and Agility

In her book *The Silo Effect: The Peril of Expertise and the Promise of Breaking Down Barriers,* anthropologist Gillian Tett discusses Sony's release of two new versions of the Walkman on the same day because the company's siloed organizational structure led to misalignment in product direction. "Why Sony unveiled not one, but two different digital Walkman devices in 1999," she writes, "was because it was completely fragmented: different departments of the Sony empire had each developed their own—different—digital music devices . . . None of these departments, or silos, was able to agree on a single product approach, or even communicate with each other to swap ideas, or agree on a joint strategy."[34] The lesson here is that despite bringing in the right skills and allowing these skills to flourish, functional silos can kill innovation and product strategy.

Innovation tends to flourish in cross-functional teams because these teams have more diversity of perspective and can act more rapidly to develop and test product ideas. "Squad" structures work especially well as a model

---

33 Pulakos, E. and Kaiser, R. (April 7, 2020). *To Build an Agile Team, Commit to Organizational Stability. Harvard Business Review.*
34 Boss, J. (September 18, 2017). *Silos Are Killing Amazon's Potential. Don't Let Them Kill Yours. Forbes.*

for effective cross-functional teams. Born from the digital-first world (which leads the way in building agile organizations), a squad refers to a small group of people chosen from different areas of the organization. Each person owns different parts of the process but they come together to tackle a particular problem, project, challenge, or product. People can come on or off the team depending on the situational need. Squads are nimble and flexible, crucial attributes for operating in an innovative world.

As an example, in order to support their strategy of developing and selling more scalable products, Relevate is moving away from functional silos to multi-functional teams that are smaller and composed of more "T-shaped" people (individuals who have the breadth of skill, but depth in one particular area). Reorganizing around multi-functional teams has been a year-long journey for Relevate, beginning with training on Agile working methods, moving on to a pilot multi-functional team, and then finally, a broader roll-out.

Company-Wide Technical Acumen

In addition to skilled cross-functional teams, company-wide technical acumen, also known as digital fluency, is required. Everyone in the organization—from the CEO to the intern—needs to be digitally fluent. Digital fluency is a combination of both understanding and appropriately using technology. In the simplest example, digital fluency isn't knowing how to build a database, it's knowing what data belongs in a database and how to enter data into it and pull reports out of it. Boston Consulting Group (BCG) accurately describes the importance of digital fluency. "If the growth in digital talent outpaces the ability of the rest of the workforce to keep up, the company as a whole will be left behind."[35]

35 *Strack, R., Dyrchs, S., Kotsis, A. and Mingardon, S. (2017). How to Gain and*

We can build technical acumen through standard classroom and self-serve training methods; we can also simply start using more digital tools, as most workplaces have had to do during COVID-19. The more digital exposure employees have, the more likely they are to adapt and to begin the intuitive process of understanding other digital products.

A Test-and-Learn Mindset

Last, but definitely not least, organizations need to develop a test-and-learn mindset that is applied at every stage of the product development process. A test-and-learn mindset is so important that it's a central part of the product innovation loop and MVP approach introduced earlier in this book, and a topic that will be revisited throughout. As a reminder, an MVP is the easiest product to build that meets assumptions about customers' needs and allows us to gather as much data as possible to confirm (or correct) those assumptions. Or, as *Lean Startup* creator Eric Ries explains, it's an integral part of a build, measure, learn loop.

The MVP is a version of a product (or product idea) with the right balance of features to satisfy early customers and provide learning opportunities. An MVP is not a smaller, cheaper version of a final product; it is a version of the product containing the minimum number of features making it cost-effective to deploy while still allowing us to test our product in real-life situations, thus validating the product's core value. MVP tests are designed to answer technical questions about the product, prove or disprove hypotheses, and get a real feel for the viability of the product in the market.

Develop Digital Talent and Skills. BCG: Boston.

A key point to remember is that an MVP shouldn't be released without a vision that details the future plans of the product. Product roadmaps are used to set the course from MVP to future product releases. They serve to chart long-term product direction from the MVP stage onward, requiring frequent updates based on the information learned in the build, measure, learn loop process.

Clear and detailed testing plans for the first few releases are also necessary. It's important to have a process in place for documenting open questions and key hypotheses, as well as defining how they'll be tested. Additionally, a well-defined process for capturing data and for revisiting hypotheses will ensure a "learn and adapt as we go" approach.

It's important that testing focuses on how customer needs can be better served and not just on how to improve the features of a product. This means that experiments should focus on things such as why the customer uses the product, how they use it, what they would do differently, etc., as well as questions about the ease of use and overall functionality.

Finally, it is necessary to be very explicit with sales teams and customers that methods are part of an iterative process. It should be stated up front that changes will be made to the product as more people begin to use it, and that feedback will be encouraged so that the product can continue to meet consumers' needs.

Test-and-learn product design is a new way of working for many of us, but the payoff can be huge. A recent survey of 170 executives who work in R&D, strategy, and new product development roles at large public companies found agreement on several benefits of the test-and-learn product design approach:

- Speed! A faster cycle time for developing ideas.

- Making decisions based on evidence and data rather than executives' instincts.

- Better quality feedback from customers and stakeholders—often because we're asking them to actually buy and use something rather than just spout opinions in a focus group.

- "Getting out of the building" to personally speak to and observe customers and stakeholders.

- More flexibility around making changes to ideas as they progress from concept to MVP to finished product.[36]

Many leaders and organizations struggle to adopt a test-and-learn approach because it requires changing the standards of what "done" looks like. It also requires the building of capabilities to quickly collect, aggregate, interpret, and apply customer feedback to the MVP (and future versions) to speed up product evolution. Testing and learning, at speed, takes a lot of work. It also takes highly specialized analytical skills and a deep understanding of smart product development. This is where many organizations benefit from outside help.

Altering company culture is another area where help from outside experts can be beneficial. As Simon Frewer said about Challenger's shift to a more product-led culture: "As we moved from pure service to more product-led tech-enabled services, using outside help and getting feedback on our team's capabilities was really important . . . Don't underestimate how big of a change management effort it is for internal staff across the entire organization to move from pure services to tech-enabled services or products."

---

36 *Innovation Leader (n.d.) How Large Organizations are Deploying Lean Startup.*

Action Steps

1. How will a scalable product and solutions strategy increase your organization's impact on customers?

2. Catalog your leadership team's capabilities: do you have people with product skills and digital fluency?

3. Rate your own readiness to "test-and-learn" on a scale of 1 to 10, with 1 being "not at all ready" and 10 being "already doing it."

The Productize Pathway

Chapter Four

MISTAKE: Favoring Core Businesses, Rather Than New Products
SOLUTION: Align to Support Innovation

Christophe Martel is the CEO and Co-Founder of TI-People, Inc., an employee experience design and intelligence company. When COVID-19 hit, he and his partner Volker Jacobs saw an opportunity to accelerate the creation of recurring revenue streams through subscription products as opposed to relying on customized services.

Consulting and design services had been funding the business; however, many consulting projects were put on hold with the onset of COVID-19, creating a "burning platform" to migrate the business to a product-centric model. Christophe and Volker knew that their most important challenge was to get the leadership team aligned around a product strategy.

To begin with, the team had to acknowledge that the palette of customer needs in the employee experience market was much too broad to cover in its entirety; leaving behind many superficially attractive opportunities was the key to victory on specific battlegrounds. A senior group of leaders with a divergent mix of experiences and backgrounds (experience design, management consulting, scaled information, and technology businesses) had to converge on the company's product niche (where they would focus) and periphery (where they would no longer focus). Each leadership team member was asked to independently produce a write-up that answered four questions:

- What type of business do we want to be?
- Why do we want to do this?
- What does success look like?
- What's the one thing we want to be known for by our customers and investors?

This exercise helped the team coalesce the different interpretations of what the business should become so that the alignment process could begin. Shared personal analyses gave each leader a deeper understanding of the others' starting points, allowing them all to eventually meet at the same destination.

That kind of alignment in mindset is essential. In this chapter, I'll explore other strategies for aligning productization strategy within your organization. And I'll discuss how to set yourself up for success by aligning budgets and incentives around a product strategy.

As I discussed in the last chapter, creating a specific, targeted vision—such as the target number of organizations served, or the target percentage of revenue from new products—is a good place to begin envisioning goals. But after that, it's necessary to point your organization's efforts in the direction of that vision. This means deciding how much to invest in developing, launching, and maintaining new products, and appropriately measuring these investments. This involves:

- Aligning the shareholders and executive team

- Determining how much to invest

- Deciding how to allocate investments

- Freeing up resources

- Aligning incentives

Aligning Shareholders and the Executive Team

RevJen provides nonprofit sector leaders with executive peer groups and training that is focused on improving revenue generation capabilities. Brian Joseph, CEO and Founding Partner, initially founded RevJen as a consulting business, but he quickly learned that while it could be lucrative, his vision regarding the company's potential impact was limited. He wouldn't be able to quickly scale the consulting services he provided, which meant less exposure in the nonprofit sector. He also knew he'd rather have a business that was one-to-many rather than one built on advising organizations one-to-one.

So, as Brian describes it, he decided to "burn the boats" and take the leap from a consulting business model to a product business model. Brian's first step was to have a discussion with his founding partners about the new direction of the company. Through these conversations, they reached an amicable solution where two partners decided to leave and one stayed to help manifest the new direction of the organization. Next, Brian had to decide what type of business model and product to build. He and his founding partner settled on building a training product, but they did not have expertise in designing and building an effective training product. He began talking to everyone he knew, using the power of networking, to find and bring in the development help he needed.

Completely shutting down the services side of the business is not a strategy most organizations should or are able to utilize; however, Brian's experience illustrates the commitment required to build and launch products successfully. As Simpact CEO Dejan Duzevik put it, a line in the sand may need to be drawn. "You may have to fire some customers that are with you for your services. You can't sit in two chairs and pretend you are a service company with them, but be building products."

Whether we are burning boats, drawing a line in the sand, or taking on some other form of commitment, it's vital that your team is as ready as you are to take the leap. Andrew Stockwell, former SVP Research Product & Operations at Lux Research (with similar product experience at Forrester Research and Kantar) says that organizations migrating to a product strategy thrive when there is sufficient trust among the executive team to allow for productive conflict about fundamental business questions. That said, Andrew states that, "even if there is disagreement, it's essential to get enough alignment that you come out of that meeting with one voice and one message that everyone rigorously sticks to that governs our strategy around product-market fit."

Determining How Much to Invest

Many services businesses first fund products that they can sell to a single client as part of an engagement. While that is a tempting strategy, those products tend to fail because the primary focus is the needs of one client as opposed to the needs of the larger market. To increase the chance of success in productizing services, product development typically needs to be funded out of profit.

The most successful organizations put aside a small amount of investment to discover market needs, define the right customer problem to solve, test potential products that will solve those problems, and test hypotheses about market potential and the additional investment required to build a product. Depending on company size, 2 to 3 percent of revenue is a good place to start for this exploration investment.

There are relatively inexpensive and fast ways to start investing. For example, Empower has been on a product journey for the last 5 years. Jim Price started the journey by first creating the Empower Explorer Program. *Explorers* are 3-person teams of employees who, in addition to their day jobs, spend 6 months finding opportunities at the periphery of the business. In return, they receive a small stipend of $3,000 on top of their salaries. The Explorer program was a great way to kick off new product innovation at Empower without significant up-front investment. Since the Explorer program launched, investment has grown substantially to include development resources, a Chief Product Officer, and a Product Innovation Council focused exclusively on allocating investments across the innovation pipeline.

Eventually, the product exploration budget should grow to include new product development, which typically ranges from 10 to 30 percent of revenue, depending on the types of products built.[37] For organizations adopting a productization strategy for growth, the size of the budget typically depends on the amount of digital disruption a company is facing. It's important to note that research studies have found no relationship between the size of the innovation budget and innovation success.[38] What matters is how effectively the budget is managed.

---

37 Ahlawat, P, et al. (2019). *How Software Companies Can Get More Bang for Their R&D Buck.* Boston, MA: Boston Consulting Group.
38 Staack, V. and Cole, B. (2017). *Reinventing Innovation: Five Findings to Guide Strategy Through Execution.* PwC.

Deciding How to Allocate Investments

At this stage, it's also critical to develop a straw man for how new product ideas, once explored, will be evaluated for further investment. In other words, what criteria will be used to decide whether ideas get additional funding? These can be as simple or as complicated as desired.

I recommend creating a one-page strategy overview for each idea that includes answers to the following questions:

- **Vision:** What is the purpose behind the solution? What positive change should it bring about for the users and buyers?

- **Target Group:** Who are the target buyers and users?

- **Customer Needs:** What urgent and expensive customer problem does the solution solve?

- **Solution:** What are the primary features of the solution? What makes it stand out from alternative offerings?

- **Business Goals:** What are the business goals (e.g., revenue, new customers, improved profitability, etc.)?

Please note that the answers to most of these questions will be hypothetical at this stage. Through the iterative test-and-learn approach to new product development, these hypotheses will be tested.

The leadership team will need to agree on what criteria to use to score and prioritize ideas. Metrics such as the revenue potential (near-term and longer-term), the payback period, and the ability to attract new customers might be some factors considered. The team also needs to agree on a precise definition of each criterion. For example, if one of the metrics is "ability to implement," then how is this assessed? Time to implement?

Level of change required? The number of new capabilities needed? All of the above? If the definitions are not clear and agreed upon, the "scores" for each product are meaningless.

For organizations that are just getting started, a straightforward framework for evaluating ideas is recommended. Many organizations look at Revenue, Confidence, and Effort which is a variation of the RICE method[39] (Reach, Impact, Confidence, and Effort). The simplified method includes:

- Revenue: an estimate of sales with assumptions around price and volume.

- Confidence level: how sure are you that the idea will yield the estimated revenue? (High = 100 percent, Medium = 75 percent, Low = 50 percent)

- Effort: how much time, money, and other resources will it take to create and sell the product? A simplified way of looking at this is how many "person-months" will be involved? (Use whole numbers and a minimum of half a month.)

To get the score, multiply Revenue by Confidence and then divide that number by the Effort.

Once every idea is scored, results can be tabulated and prioritized:

Product	Revenue	Confidence	Effort	Score
Idea 1	12,000	80	12	80,000
Idea 2	600	100	3	20,000
Idea 3	5,000	80	6	66,667

---

39 *Product Plan (n.d.). RICE Scoring Method. https://www.poductplan.com/glossary/rice-scoring-model/*

Building your own scoring model is fair game too. I recently coached one company through a new product prioritization exercise. We started with a very long list of potential evaluation criteria, narrowed the list down to the most critical elements, and then created a weighted value for each metric. In this case, the ability to land new customers was weighed more highly than the payback period. We also created a 2-step process to eliminate ideas that didn't meet a set of "litmus tests" before scoring began. The litmus test included things such as market size and gross margins above 80 percent.

Criteria can include anything important to business goals; 3 possible examples are new customer acquisition, margin improvement, or revenue growth. Some organizations weigh each criterion in order to rank their importance. For a scoring system to work well, the leadership team must be aligned in terms of how criteria are defined.

After scoring each idea, it's useful to visualize the portfolio of options to see where the best options are, and also to see if a well-balanced portfolio has been created. An easy way to do this is to plot the ideas on a matrix with complexity along one axis and business value along the other. Annualized revenue or profit, a third dimension, could be represented by the size of the bubble. This matrix is divided into four quadrants to help determine areas of prioritization:

Value-Complexity Matrix

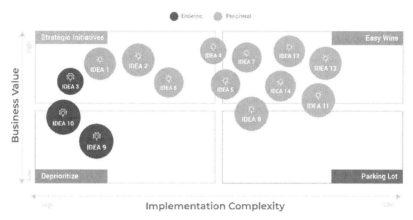

Ideas with low business value and high complexity are deprioritized. Ideas with high value and low complexity are immediately pursued, as are longer-term payoff ideas with high value, but also higher complexity.

It's worth noting that evaluating new product ideas as part of existing operational budgeting forums won't work because new products will always lose out in investment terms to existing products and services. Creating a product innovation governance group to discuss funding and provide stakeholders with regular updates about new product development can be very useful. Empower's Product Innovation Council is a good example. The Council meets regularly to assess the company's product investments across three innovation pipelines: Endemic, Independent, and Leveraged. Endemic products can be folded into work with existing clients. Independent products are adjacent to existing services and are run as separate brands (e.g., ClearTrade, a tech-enabled media buying solution). Leveraged products are completely outside the core business, but still leverage the skills of existing employees (e.g., Tanon Leather Goods, an online leather goods retailer). The Council monitors the performance of current products and assesses new ideas, which keeps innovation decisions one step removed from operational budget decisions.

To effectively allocate new product investment dollars, the leadership team needs to decide what percentage of new product development funds will be spent on "easy win" ideas versus more strategic or transformational ideas. Recent benchmarking research from KPMG found that the best innovators are spending more of their innovation budgets on transformational innovation as compared to less successful innovators.[40] In fact, the most successful innovators allocate 37 percent of their portfolio to more strategic, transformational innovation.

Establishing a regular cadence of reviewing the progress of different ideas and reallocating funds based on new information is recommended. As we learn more about the market and product development requirements, the scores for each new product idea will change. Monthly meetings to review the initial portfolio are recommended. Once there's an established portfolio of both existing and new products, quarterly meetings are sufficient.

At this stage, it's also common to choose an axis of growth. In other words, which market segmentation scheme best supports a scalable product? Is it anchored by geography? By industry? By function? Whatever segmentation scheme we select, the TAM of each market segment will need to be large enough to support the development and maintenance of a scalable product. Is the TAM large enough to yield a good return on the product investment?

When choosing the axis for scale, it's necessary to take into account how common the needs are across customers in the segment. It's important

---

40 Grandi, F., Drummond, C., and Bolen, R. (2020). *Benchmarking Innovation Impact 2020. Innovation Leader and KPMG.*

that there is an opportunity for a product that scales across multiple customers so that we don't fall back into providing customized services due to highly variable, individual customer needs.

🛠 PRODUCT STRATEGY TEMPLATE

🛠 PRODUCT PORTFOLIO SCORING TEMPLATE

🛠 PRODUCT PORTFOLIO MATRIX TEMPLATE
(Visit *www.theproductizebook.com* to download the tools.)

Freeing Up Resources

Organizations have a variety of options to fund product exploration, including reducing returns to shareholders, taking on new investors through debt or equity, and even having existing clients partially fund development through engagements that include products. Partnering is another funding path. Another often overlooked way to free up resources for new product investment is to reduce the amount of customization in existing work.

By reducing customization of existing products or customization within engagements, additional investment can be made into new product development. Existing products or productized services and requests for customization can be a significant resource drain for product development teams. In fact, reducing custom development requests is the largest challenge for companies seeking to migrate from customized solutions to more standardized products. Customization is often promised by well-meaning sales or account management teams that don't fully understand the value of a more scalable product strategy. However, if a team is spending all of their time on custom requests, they will never have the time to make the scalable products successful.

One company tackled the problem of customized development requests in less than 9 months. After decades of success selling product management training services that were often heavily customized, the firm Strategy Execution (a project management training company now owned by global HR consultancy Korn Ferry) decided they needed to build more scalable, technology-based training products to effectively compete in a changing market. They did not have new investment dollars to fund building more scalable products, so they diverted their existing product development teams away from customized work and toward building scalable products.

The shift started with both the CEO and the Head of Sales announcing the strategy change at the annual sales kick-off. Knowing that they could not flip a switch and completely stop custom work for clients, they created a way for the sales and account management team to request an exception on behalf of a client. This came in the form of a "customization ticket" that was first reviewed by the product team and ultimately decided upon by the Head of Sales and the CEO (if necessary). When completing this customized work request ticket, the submitter had to outline a simple business case:

- Which client? The decision-makers needed to know the overall seriousness of the situation. Is this a large, established client with a minor request? Or is this a new client with a huge request?

- Then there was the money factor to consider.

  o How much overall engagement will there be with this client?

  o How much is this specific opportunity worth?

- Is the client prepared to spend money on the work to be done for the customization (i.e., can it be priced with full margin back to ensure all direct costs are covered)?

- When do they need this by (in terms of both the answer and the work)?

- What is the "guaranteed" revenue in the next twelve months?

- What is the specific request? What customization work do they actually want?

Once Strategy Execution began implementing this process, many requests that might have been fulfilled before were automatically dismissed because of a lack of a positive ROI. It's a lot easier to assess the value of a customization request when it is written down. The big help, especially for the sales team engagement, was that it wasn't the product development team saying "no"—it was the leadership team, including the Head of Sales, saying "no."

Strategy Execution started with a goal of no more than 25 percent of the total product development team's effort being spent on custom projects. Originally, the team was at about 40 percent. But 5 months after they set the goal, the average was about 15 to 20 percent, representing a 50 percent decline. Saying "no" to clients isn't always easy, which is why it's essential to put a process together for building the case to say "no."

Aligning Incentives

David Evans is Chief Product Officer of Collage Group, a customer insight research firm on a productization journey, focused on understanding the cultural transformation of the American consumer driven by the rapid growth of the multicultural population. He explains that one of the hardest things to do in moving to scalable products is figuring out how to "disentangle the claws of time and materials billing." In consulting businesses, the urgent priorities of the client and the chance to realize cash more quickly tend to crowd out the time needed to develop a productized business, no matter how strategic the change might be. These conflicting incentives pit the consulting business against productization. "Unit pricing for products, especially subscription products, tends to be so much lower than what you get as a consultant for a project, and it accrues slowly. Cash from the non-scalable consulting dollar saves our bacon, but it can be a false promise," David described.

That brings me to another important aspect of alignment: incentives. Teams will need to be incentivized to sell lower-ticket, standardized products as opposed to the high-ticket consulting engagements. Incentives can be achieved through higher commissions on product sales, to cite one example. Christoffer Ellehuus, the CEO of Strategy Execution, shared how he changed incentives for the sales team during his company's product transition. Salespeople received a 3 percent commission on consulting engagements and 6 percent on subscription product sales. "It's not about telling people they can't do something. It's about putting enough barriers and meaningful incentives in place to move them in the direction you want," Christoffer shared.

Ultimately, as David Evans puts it, "It's going to come down to a very deliberate decision to say no to things. The question we have to ask ourselves is when we can say no to cash-rich consulting engagements valued at one times revenue vs lower subscription product revenue valued at four to six times revenue. If we can't say no at that point of equivalent value, we are either not taking our strategy seriously, or we need an interim solution that reduces the conflicts from closing consulting deals."

Collage moved the split between consulting new business and subscription new business from 50/50 in 2019 to 10/90 in 2020. To get there, they had to build a rigorous foundation that changed the value of the data and content embedded in the product from "nice to have" to "need to have." This strengthened renewal rates, inspiring commercial teams away from defaulting to consulting engagements. The kicker came at the end of 2020 when responding to a significant consulting RFP from a major consumer products company that would have distracted from the subscription product business. The decision was made to substantially reduce the incentives in 2021 for closing consulting deals, formally setting the precedent for "saying no" to such RFPs in the future.

Action Steps

1. List the criteria for evaluating new opportunities. Are they equally weighted? Which ones are most important for making progress against your longer-term strategy for the organization?

2. Consider the options for freeing up resources for innovation investment. Which option is most feasible?

3. Put processes in place to regularly evaluate your progress against your productization strategy and your innovation portfolio. At the very least, schedule a recurring monthly meeting to review.

PART TWO

FOLLOW URGENT, EXPENSIVE PROBLEMS

"If I had an hour to solve a problem, I'd spend 55 minutes thinking about the problem and 5 minutes thinking about solutions."

– attributed to Albert Einstein

The Productize Pathway

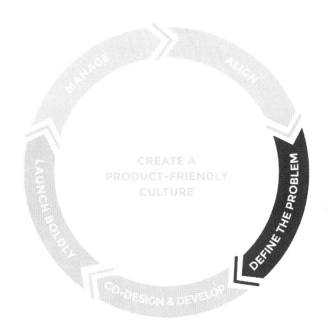

Chapter Five

MISTAKE: Developing Products That Don't Solve an Urgent & Expensive Problem
SOLUTION: Define the Right Problem

A client recently asked me: "What's the biggest new product development mistake you see companies make?" I immediately said, "Developing a product that does not solve an urgent and expensive customer problem."

The goal of the **Define the Problem** phase is to avoid this mistake. The best products start with a clear understanding of the market. This includes:

- Understanding our customers' urgent and expensive problems

- Knowing how these problems present by different segments or personas

- Understanding the competitive landscape

Understanding our customers—or more specifically, their urgent and expensive problems—is the key to developing a successful product. Too many companies waste time developing a new product that no customer wants or needs. Take, for example, Pepsi Crystal, New Coke, or the lesser-known flop, "Satisfries" from Burger King. In 2013, Burger King introduced Satisfries as a healthy alternative to their traditional french fries. They made two poor assumptions when developing the new product. First, they assumed that customers wanted healthier fries, and second, that they'd be willing to pay more for them; neither of these assumptions turned out to be true. As a result, Burger King discontinued the fries less than a year after they were introduced.

There are several reasons why an organization might develop a product that does not solve an urgent and expensive problem. Sometimes, companies fall into the trap of creating products they can't sell when they overfocus on leveraging existing intellectual property. Building a product around unique, protectable IP is appealing because leveraging existing IP lowers the effort required to create a product. However, the product still needs to solve an urgent and expensive customer problem.

Similarly, companies can get excited about what a competitor is doing and copy that competitor without pausing to ask if the competitor is successfully meeting a customer need. Without putting in the work to understand our customers, we risk replicating our competitors' mistakes, not their successes.

All too often, a product is developed to address a *common* problem, but not an *urgent and expensive* customer problem. Clayton Christensen's advice to design products that solve customers' "jobs-to-be-done" is frequently cited among product innovation professionals. He suggests looking for ". . . poorly performed 'jobs' in customers' lives and then design[ing] products, experiences, and processes around those jobs."[41] However, finding a "job-to-be-done" is not enough. I encourage clients

41 Christensen, C. M., Hall, T., Dillon, K., & Duncan, D. S. (2016). *Know our customers' "jobs to be done." Harvard Business Review, 94(9),*14

to find an *urgent and expensive* job-to-be-done. It's critical to understand the difference between a minor annoyance and a real pain point. Solving a minor annoyance will "improve people's moods but not their lives."[42] For example, a head of HR might be annoyed that staff are not taking advantage of online courses that are available to them, but a real pain point for her is finding and retaining people who already have the right skills.

Organizations also fail when they develop a product that addresses a *symptom* of a problem, not a *root cause*. A classic example comes from a major airline that commonly heard complaints from flyers about flight delays. Their own data showed that their planes were leaving on time more often than would be assumed from the number of complaints and low ratings customers were giving the airline. When the airline dug deeper, they discovered that the real issue wasn't the delays, it was the communication—or lack thereof—about delays. To address the issue, the airline worked to ensure that flight delay communication was consistent and met customer expectations.

Another mistake is confusing the current solution with the problem. Consider this oft-cited example from Harvard Business School marketing professor, Theodore Levitt. A potential customer needs a hole in their wall to hang a painting. The current solution to that problem is a drill. We might be tempted to create a better drill, but if we take a step back to reconsider the problem (a hole is needed in a wall) we could design an entirely new way to create better holes in walls. As Levitt puts it, "People don't want to buy a quarter-inch drill. They want a quarter-inch hole!"

Mobility—getting from point A to point B—provides another similar example. When cars were invented, people stopped buying horses and buggies; it no longer mattered how fast the horses were or how good the

---

42 Sawhney, M. S. (2016). *Putting products into services. Harvard Business Review, 94(9) 82*

buggies were, people wanted cars. The customer issue was mobility, not slow horses. Car companies are facing a similar market disruption to that felt by the horse and buggy companies. The urgent and expensive problem that cars solve is getting from point A to point B. Enter Uber and Lyft, two companies that innovatively solve that problem while leaving car manufacturers out of the loop.

 ## Customer Needs Identification Worksheet
(visit *www.theproductizebook.com* to download the tools.)

There are things we can do to avoid solving the wrong problem. Adopting a simple, hypothesis-based research approach to understanding both customer needs and how competitors are already addressing those needs is recommended.

Step One: Develop hypotheses to test

Step Two: Understand the competitive landscape

Step Three: Test hypotheses using tools such as:

- Customer and prospect interviews
- Surveys
- Customer advisory boards
- Online data
- Existing product data

Step One: Develop Hypotheses to Test

Start by outlining:

- Hypotheses about customers' urgent and expensive problems
- Types of customer segments experiencing these problems
- How customers are currently solving those problems

To begin the hypotheses process, think about questions such as:

- What is the main problem?
- What is the root of the problem?
- Are customers satisfied with current solutions?
- Which customer segments or personas have this problem?
- How much value do customers receive in solving that problem?
- Can our product idea solve that problem?

A testable hypothesis should state the problem and what we expect the solution to achieve. For example:

- I believe [target market] will [do this action/use this solution] for [this reason].
- Because I believe [this is a problem], if I offer [this solution], I expect [this result] to happen.

Sakichi Toyoda, a Japanese inventor and industrialist, developed the "five whys" root cause analysis method to provide a better understanding of any problem and help uncover its solution. It's a simple process that involves asking the question, "why" enough times to get past symptoms of a problem to the root cause. The point is not to stay anchored to a particular solution or surface-level problem. Recalling the airline's experience of digging deeper to understand the real problem, the root cause of customer dissatisfaction wasn't departure delays; it was the airline's inconsistent communication around departure delays. Scenarios like this show that understanding the root of our customers' problems is the only way to develop an effective product solution.

SAMPLE ROOT CAUSE ANALYSIS
(visit *www.theproductizebook.com* to download the tools.)

It's important to hypothesize which segments or customer personas have the problem. A segment could be derived from market characteristics such as large company/small company, existing client/new client, US/ International, or other specific industry. As was mentioned in Chapter Four on Alignment, knowing which segment has each problem is critical to ensuring that the Total Addressable Market (TAM) is large enough to support a product strategy. If a segment is too small to yield a strong return with a product developed specifically for them, it's worth exploring the idea of serving that smaller segment with a more generic product and different marketing messaging. For example, it may not make economic sense to create an industry-specific version of a product designed for corporate finance departments, but industry-specific marketing messaging for the product could be developed.

A persona is a fictional character created to represent a potential buyer of the product and a potential user of the product. For example, one buyer type might be a new human resources head, and one user type might be an employee who goes through training that the new head of human resources just purchased. Personas include detailed descriptions of the personal attributes, such as where the person works and lives, family status, interests, stressors, even a quote they might live by—anything that provides insight into this fictional character's motivations and buying decisions. Keeping with our human resources scenario, the following example using "Michelle" illustrates just how detailed personas should be.

Michelle – VP, Talent Development/Management

Michelle is 49 (but embracing 50!). She's married and has 2 teenagers at home. Her husband works, but she has the bigger job.

Michelle is not on the Exec team, but she has access to its members. Many women in the company look up to her. At times she can feel overwhelmed, but she has a great support network. She wants to be considered a leader.

She's savvy and well-dressed. Her family and faith are important to her. She reads the NYT, HBR, industry mags, and follows a few mom blogs. She active on FB as it relates to her family and has a LinkedIn account she doesn't have time for.

Buying Behavior

She solves problems in a decisive, active and assertive manner and doesn't include people in the decision-making process that she doesn't see as vital. She's proactive, results driven and wants to win. She might seem pushy and demanding and wants things to happen on her timeframe.

Purchase Goals

Credibility matters. She has budget responsibility and is eager to show how she can help her company produce better results by maximizing talent. Even though she's 'taught and bought' it all, she chooses a vendor because they have made her look good, proactively help her, and take a lot off her plate.

It's important to catalog all of our hypotheses so that we can track our learnings against them. A simple excel spreadsheet works to list all the hypotheses and any data that either proves or disproves them. When working with one company, my team brainstormed approximately thirty hypotheses with the client. About half were related to the urgent and expensive customer problem, the remainder were related to the product concept. Throughout the project, we came back to these hypotheses to see what we had validated, what we had disproven, what no longer applied, and what we still needed to uncover. Our evolving list of hypotheses shaped our interview guides, surveys, and overall research approach.

Step Two: Understanding the Competitive Landscape

After creating numerous hypotheses, the next step is to gain a better understanding of competitors serving the target market segments.

Before diving into the fundamentals of good competitive analysis, I want to mention that I wholeheartedly agree with Tara-Nicholle Nelson, former VP of Marketing for MyFitnessPal, who said "The question is not *who* our competition is but *what* it is. And the answer is this: Our competition is any and every obstacle our customers encounter along their journeys to solving the human, high level problems our company exists to solve."[43]

In the case of MyFitnessPal, competition is anything that makes it harder to live a healthy life. Their competitors don't just include companies like Weight Watchers. They're also up against the fact that healthy food is more expensive and more inconvenient than junk food, and that people have a natural, biological craving for fat. This scenario illustrates the important point that a focus on traditional competitors leads to "me too" products rather than true breakthrough ideas.

Widening this lens also helps us identify new entrants who are serving the same customers and addressing the same problems, but with completely different solutions. This means that digital-first start-ups may emerge on our competitor scan. For example, a search and staffing company was considering a large investment in a new product and wanted my team to research new digital-only entrants, not their traditional competitors. They needed to understand how well these new entrants were solving the same customer problem, but with a completely different approach. Going back to a previous example, when the customer problem is mobility, a competitor to General Motors is not just Ford, but also Uber or Lyft.

43 Nicholle-Nelson, T. (May 11, 2017) *Obsess Over Your Customers, Not Your Rivals. Harvard Business Review.*

To identify digital-first start-ups serving our target market, resources such as CB Insights, Owler, and Capterra are useful. Advisors, investors, and a few customer interviews are also great sources for competitive information. Start with an exhaustive list of everyone in the space, but then cut the list down to just a handful of the companies that seem to best address the hypothesized urgent and expensive problems.

Once you have a shortlist of traditional and non-traditional competitors, dive deep into each one. Secondary sources are suitable for a first dive into the tangible and intangible assets, capabilities, niche, and current market positions. Check news coverage (mainstream and business press), annual reports, or one of the many business databases (such as Hoovers). Social media and company websites also reveal a lot about brand identity and marketing strategies. Sign up for competitors' newsletters and review their job postings and LinkedIn profiles to see where they are making talent investments.

Here are some key questions to answer: Are our competitors efficiently solving our customers' most urgent and expensive problems? Where is the white space to solve customer problems not currently being addressed by our competitors, or by do-it-yourself alternatives?

Typical competitive analysis is about developing a rich understanding of who is doing what in our market space. It answers questions such as:

- What is each competitor's value proposition and positioning?
- What products or services do they sell? Features? Benefits?
- What is each competitor's profile (number of employees, revenue, public/private, etc.)?
- What is each competitor's market share?
- Who is each competitor's target market/audience/user?

- How do they market their products or services?

- What are their strengths and weaknesses?

- What potential threats do our competitors pose?

- How do they plan to grow in the future?

- How do they package and price their products?

- What potential opportunities do they make available (where is the white space)?

Once the data is collected, the hypotheses will need to be adjusted based on what has been learned. Moving forward, continued monitoring of our competitors through the rest of the productization journey will also be required. Refresh your competitor analysis quarterly, and consider tracking metrics that speak to:

- Company health, i.e., changes in company size (revenue and employees), changes in primary investors, new patents, etc.

- Key product performance metrics from the customer perspective (price, quality, delivery, ease of use)

- New product launches

- Marketing strategies, i.e., content channels and content quality

 COMPETITOR RESEARCH CHECKLIST

 COMPETITOR COMPARISON GRID

 COMPETITOR ANALYSIS TEMPLATES
(visit *www.theproductizebook.com* to download the tools.)

Step Three: Test Customer Problem Hypotheses

Now that hypotheses have been developed and refined, and there's a clear understanding of the competitive landscape, the last step in **Define the Problem** is to test these hypotheses. There are multiple ways to do this. My favorite approaches for B2B products are:

- Customer and prospect interviews
- Customer advisory boards
- Surveys
- Online data analysis
- Existing product usage data analysis

Interviews and advisory boards can be time-consuming, but both of these approaches are incredibly useful when asking follow-up questions in order to understand problems or dig deep into existing solutions. Interviews and boards are also good for getting in-depth feedback on potential product concepts; they help in the evolution of ideas because discussion guides or concepts can be iterated after each conversation. In other words, these mediums are useful for helping us understand "why" customers have the problems they do, as well as helping us test multiple hypotheses around "how" we might solve those customer problems.

Surveys are useful when trying to achieve certainty around the attributes of a specific segment, the willingness to pay, and preferences for different features. Surveys have a role to play in pressure-testing financial projections and collecting information when limited time is available.

In other words, surveys convey "what" buyers and users are likely to do or prefer.

Analyzing existing product usage data or analyzing online search data is helpful to understand how buyers and users *actually* behave, whereas interviews and surveys will tell us how they *might* behave. These types of data analysis can validate what we learn through other research methods or identify discrepancies between believed behavior and actual behavior. Existing data analysis is also good for gaining a high-level understanding of where opportunities might come from, making such methods useful in the beginning phases of research.

Let's look at each testing method in more detail.

Test Hypotheses: Customer and Prospect Interviews

Although interviews can be time-consuming, they yield the deepest insights. And if you do them well, you don't need to do that many.

Whom to Interview

There isn't time to talk to everyone, so you'll need to lean on segments and personas in order to interview a mix of people. Assuming three or four target segments, the necessary data can be gleaned from ten to twelve interviews (three to four interviews per segment). It is really about quality over quantity.

If the new product is intended to bring in new clients, make sure to have prospects in the interview mix. If the product could be received differently by very mature versus less mature customers, then have a mix of both. Also, consider if there will be differences in needs between the end user and buyers. For example, if selling a training product, you'll want to interview both the buyers (a department head, a learning and development executive, etc.) and users (employees who would undergo the training).

Challenger's development of a new, subscription-based, online development and sales productivity product (discussed earlier) was heavily influenced by the collective voice of the customer interviews. They interviewed existing customers, lapsed customers, and prospects to identify urgent and expensive customer problems, as well as solutions their customers were already trying. CEO Simon Frewer shared that this depth of capturing customer voice and "widening the aperture" beyond existing customers allowed the leadership team to move forward with confidence in building and launching the new product. "We baked the voice of the customer learning into our product, messaging, etc. and created a value proposition that made it easy for customers to say yes."

Interview Questions

Asking the right questions is key to good research. Develop your interview guide based on the list of hypotheses in order to prove or disprove each hypothesis. Remember, the number one goal is to understand your customers' most urgent and expensive problems. You are looking to learn:

- What pain does this customer have that we can alleviate?

- What makes the problem urgent? Expensive?

- What is the root cause of the problem?

- What kinds of solutions are customers using to alleviate or get rid of the pain? How well are their solutions working?

Good questions will also eliminate interviewee bias. Questions should be as open-ended and deftly-worded as possible in order to find usable answers. Cindy Alvarez, the author of *Lean Customer Development*, has some great tips for asking the right questions in customer interviews. For example, the answer to any question that begins with, "Are you concerned about—?" will typically always be "yes," so instead, ask:

- Where are you now and where would you like to be in the future?
- What's challenging about meeting your goals?
- What would you sacrifice in order to solve a problem?
- How does X problem affect you?
- How often do you experience problem X?
- Can you tell me about the last time you experienced the problem?
- When did you last look for a solution to this problem?

Interview Logistics

You'll want to record the big insights gained from each conversation. Immediately after each interview, give the exchange a simple rating (A, B, C or 1, 2, 3) to create an "at-a-glance" look at the impact of that interviewee's comments. Later, when you've most likely forgotten the details, your notes will help to weigh the insights appropriately and guide you as to where to focus your analysis. Track big "a-ha" moments as they come up; the more we hear a particular key insight, the more weight it gets in the analysis. Hopefully, these key insights track to your hypotheses, but occasionally, something surprising pops up.

Return to your list of hypotheses after each interview. What is the most expensive, urgent problem that people are facing? Can you solve that problem? Are you creating enough value for customers to jump on board? Have hypotheses been proven or disproven? Do assumptions require re-working?

Finally, after each interview, consider whether your interview guide needs to be revised. Should you tweak an opening question? Does the product description or positioning need more clarity? Can more specificity be added to our sample packaging or pricing? Don't go more than two or three interviews without adjusting the interview guide. That said, it's important to note that you shouldn't fully abandon an idea or make big adjustments too soon. Tweaking and modifying is valuable because it helps us learn, but modifications should never be based on one person's opinion. The rule of thumb for good research is to hear something from at least two people before making a change.

 CUSTOMER INTERVIEW GUIDELINES AND QUESTIONS

 SAMPLE INTERVIEW DECK AND QUESTIONS

VOICE OF THE CUSTOMER INSIGHT TRACKING TEMPLATE
(visit *www.theproductizebook.com* to download the tools.)

Test Hypotheses: Customer Advisory Boards

A Customer Advisory Board can also provide valuable insights about a problem to be solved, as well as initial ideas for solving it. Gather individuals you think will provide honest expert opinions and use the focus group dynamic of an advisory board meeting to solicit feedback and develop ideas. Criteria can be set for who is included (such as long-term customers or customers who buy at a certain level) or strategic invitations can go out to people projected to provide valuable insights. Advisors typically aren't paid for their service, but coverage for travel expenses and meals during meetings can be supplied.

Feedback from the board meetings can be supplemented by a series of one-on-one interviews before or after the meeting. The interview process during the run-up to the advisory board meeting is similar to the process for customer and prospect interviews, but it also focuses on finding common themes for the collective group to react to in the group meeting.

 **CUSTOMER ADVISORY BOARD CREATION CHECKLIST**
(visit *www.theproductizebook.com* to download the tools.)

Test Hypotheses: Surveys

When we have very little time for research, a survey can do the job of customer interviews. The insights are not as rich, but turnaround time for a survey can be twenty-four to forty-eight hours if we already have a good list of potential respondents. Surveys are useful when a larger sample is needed to validate market potential and the size of segments. Surveys can also be useful for collecting data that can later be used in collateral or sales material.

A client that specializes in large-scale, in-person training used a survey in the very early days of the COVID-19 pandemic to better understand how their target market was reacting to the pandemic, and to get a sense of how customers' needs may have changed. The company noticed early on that many of its customers were shutting down in-person operations and limiting travel well before the local and state governments began to do so. The company sent out a survey to take the pulse of its customers and test their hypotheses about how clients planned to respond. One important thing they learned was that customers preferred to switch scheduled, live training to virtual training, rather than delay training delivery. This helped the company to quickly ramp up the resources they needed to enable virtual training delivery.

When deploying a survey, it's critical to get an adequate sample size. The way a survey is positioned to potential respondents can play a vital role in generating interest and helping to collect a sufficient amount of data. When the company in the previous example deployed their COVID-19 survey, they positioned it as a pulse benchmarking survey and offered to share the results so that each participating organization could see how their peers were responding to the pandemic and benchmark their own actions; this positioning helped to increase the response rate. It's also important to make sure respondents know how long the survey will take. Knowing exactly how much of our time we are going to give up makes it easier to agree to taking the survey.

When designing survey questions, remember that surveys are not like interviews where follow-up questions can be asked for clarification. So, when designing a survey, it's important to keep the following tips in mind:

1. *Be clear on what constitutes the "must-have" critical information.*

   It's common practice to "throw the kitchen sink" into the survey draft, rather than paring down the questions to the "must-haves." A litmus test for "must-have" information is to know how the survey data will inform decisions and next steps. If the responses to a particular question won't have any immediate actionability, the question likely isn't a must have. Keep in mind that some demographic and psychographic information will be critical if identifying different needs or preferences by customer segment is the intent.

2. *Think about user experience in the survey.*

   User experience in a survey is affected by multiple elements, including survey length, question type, page breaks, the amount of information on the screen at one time, question wording, use of design elements such as colors and fonts, and cues and instructions to provide clarity. How well a survey is designed will impact completion rates. Poor survey design makes navigation difficult for respondents and often leads to a higher drop off rate. On the other hand, a beautifully designed, but overly long survey will also engender drop off. As a general rule, surveys should be no more than ten minutes in length in order to avoid survey fatigue and drop off. Concise, well-designed surveys will almost always win the day.

3. *Word each survey with the audience in mind; don't use internal jargon.*

    This third rule should go without saying, but it's a mistake found in many surveys. The intended audience (and what they can and will understand) must always be considered when creating a survey. For example, questions aimed at theatre patrons encouraged to share their thoughts on potential productions for the upcoming season would be written with different language and tone than a survey around business growth designed for senior leaders at a Fortune 100 company. It's critical that each survey be written for the target audience, with consideration for language proficiency and level of knowledge or experience related to the survey topic. When survey takers are forced to make a guess, the accuracy of responses is jeopardized.

SAMPLE SURVEY QUESTIONS
(visit *www.theproductizebook.com* to download the tools.)

Test Hypotheses: Online data

Research can also be undertaken without ever talking to anyone by using such tools as social media ethnography and search term analysis. Ethnography entails examining people and their behaviors in a particular context and attempting to understand their thoughts and behaviors. Social media ethnography, or social listening, is the process of monitoring social media channels for mentions of a brand, competitors, products, and more. Together, LinkedIn, Twitter, Facebook, YouTube, blogs, and forums form the biggest focus group the world has ever seen; therefore, the Web contains a wealth of real-time information and insights into consumer behavior.

Let's also remember Google as it's one of the world's largest data sources. My team recently used an analysis of Google search terms to help a client think about how to prioritize potential new project management training products. There was an internal debate about whether the next new product should focus on Agile or Scrum training, or if it should focus on helping individuals earn their Project Management Professional (PMP) certification. When we looked at the twelve-month rolling average of search terms entered into Google, it was clear that interest in a PMP certification dwarfed interest in Agile or Scrum. The next step would have been to learn about the attributes of people who searched for Agile or Scrum training so that our client could use that information to build future target customer segments.

Test Hypotheses: Existing Product Data

We can learn a lot from data related to scalable solutions or products in the market. For example:

- Who buys the product? Is it heavily used? Renewable (if applicable)?

- Which features [of the product] are most heavily used?

- How do sales vary by price bands? Is discounting used? Where?

- How is financial performance? Revenue growth? Profitability? Market share?

  o If we only have customized services, it's also important to analyze the following:

- What are the types of engagements? How structured? Typical components? For whom? Average engagement size?

- How do clients concentrate across industry, maturity, title?

- What percentage of engagements have a component where the approach is heavily standardized, such as an assessment, a training session, research and analysis, etc.? How much standardization typically occurs?

- How do most clients implement the ideas or maintain the improvements?

At this point, you should have a clearly defined and well-tested hypothesis about an urgent and expensive problem to solve for customers. Now, you're ready to use the information to generate, test, and begin to develop ideas about a solution.

Action Steps

1. List the problems that you think your target market is trying to solve. Note why you think each is a problem. Did a customer

mention it? Did you read it somewhere? Is a competitor doing something related to it?

2. Note who you could ask to verify your list. Try to select a mix of current customers, prospects, and lapsed customers, as well as industry experts. Go talk to them.

The Productize Pathway

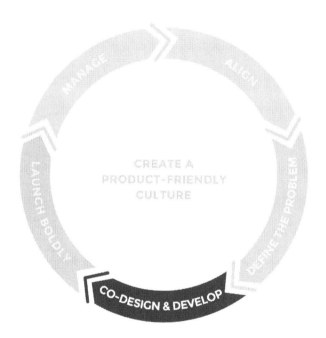

Chapter Six

MISTAKE: Designing & Developing in a Vacuum
SOLUTION: Co-Design and Develop

If Define the Problem is the most important phase, then the **Co-Design and Develop** phase is the most fun. This is where we generate, test, and develop ideas, and this phase needs to be done *after* we understand our customers' urgent and expensive problems. The best way to Co-Design and Develop is to use a co-creation model that involves ideating with employees outside of the core team, heavily engaging with potential customers, and closely partnering with developers. A co-design and develop approach allows us to keep the customers' problems at the center of our work as we go. It is based on the premise that upfront design and testing with real buyers and users will dramatically increase the likelihood of success.

This phase includes:

> **Step 1:** Cataloging existing assets
>
> **Step 2:** Developing new product ideas
>
> **Step 3:** Quickly testing product concepts with customers and prospects

Step 4: Developing preliminary business models

Step 5: Translating market requirements into product requirements that designers and developers can use to develop an MVP

Step 6: Working with designers to create and test prototypes

Step 7: Working with developers to build a functioning front-end and back-end

Step 8: Continuously soliciting user feedback

Step 1: Cataloging existing assets

A natural place to look for product ideas is in our existing intellectual property. Start by asking three questions:

1. Where is our *unique* intellectual property?

2. What data have we collected as part of our existing services?

3. What processes have we documented as part of our existing services? Where can we codify our approach?

Cataloging worked well for Linkage. When the company was transitioning to offer more scalable products, CEO Jennifer McCollum first looked at their unique intellectual property and data sets to identify opportunities for product development. "We created a productization strategy by looking at what differentiated us in a crowded industry. We had unique intellectual property around the attributes of effective leaders, and data on how best to advance women leaders. So, we built our products around these two areas because we had expertise, a unique perspective, and proprietary data to support it."

Brian Joseph at RevJen and David Evans at Collage Group both emphasize the critical value a unique framework has in creating new products. Indeed, for a new product to win out against consulting revenue, it has to be compelling enough that clients prefer sustained access to a *product* in preference to a one-time consulting *solution*. In other words, it's necessary to risk putting one's own consulting business out of business with the mining of valuable IP embedded in our product.

RevJen developed a *Revenue House* framework to explain the organizational competencies that nonprofits need to build a revenue culture. In the *Revenue House* framework, RevJen equates building revenue capacity to constructing a house:

- Setting the foundation: The foundational and strategic senior leadership decisions from which an organization builds capacity to generate revenue.

- Building the walls: The skills, processes, tools, and reporting needed for the successful day-to-day management of revenue activities.

- Finishing the roof: The skills and techniques needed for the day-to-day, frontline revenue generation.

The framework works because it's relatable, comprehensive, and unique.

Collage Group invested significantly to develop two pillars designed to help brands become "culturally fluent" in today's changing America. The framework includes two elements: first, a proprietary way to measure cultural variation across demographic groups with respect to consumer insight by category, ads, and brands. And second, a way to rank brands and ads that reveals the factors that drive the cultural fluency of marketing efforts by segment. The idea is to motivate competition among category competitors to be culturally fluent—and certainly not to be last in the ranking. The product journey went from "nice to have," as defined by insight into consumers of different demographics, to "need to have," as defined by measures of a brand's cultural fluency. Subscribing brands discover gaps they need to close in the rankings, and then use related Collage content to increase their cultural fluency.

To summarize, a good revenue culture framework:

- Helps users assess their current state (e.g., revenue weakness in the RevJen example, or ads that are missing the mark, as in the Collage Group example.)

- Articulates the ideal end state (e.g., strong revenue foundation in the case of RevJen, or a strong connection with a diverse audience for Collage Group clients.)

- Provides a roadmap for how users can get from the current state to the ideal end state.

Step 2: Developing new product ideas

There are many ways to generate potential solutions to the urgent and expensive customer problems identified in the previous chapter. Even organizations and individuals that don't consider themselves to be creative can develop a robust list of new product ideas to test. This includes looking for potential opportunities to automate, looking for service adjacencies, and gathering inspiration from other solutions.

Look for Opportunities to Automate—find solutions by looking at existing processes

Some professional services firms develop marketable products by looking for the " . . . untapped potential to automate the services they are already providing successfully," says Mohanbir Sawhney in *Putting Products into Services.*[44] In other words, what kind of technology could make delivery or use of your services easier? Sawhney provides an example of an analytics company that reviewed medical claims for fraud, waste, and abuse. Previously, this was done manually through the physical review of claims for duplicate services, miscoding, or other indicators of inappropriate billing. Over time, the company observed patterns in questionable claims. These patterns were robust enough that the company built an algorithm to detect and flag potential fraud, waste, and abuse for further review and then sold it as a SaaS product to existing and new clients.

It's worth noting that the algorithm did not eliminate the human expertise needed to examine claims thoroughly; instead, it expedited the claims review process, allowing users to significantly increase the number of claims reviewed and to flag the ones needing human review (which could be outsourced to the firm's consulting arm, or reviewed in-house).

Look for Service Adjacencies—find solutions by looking for products that enhance services

You can also look for ways to enhance or complement your services by developing adjacent products. A classic example is that of André and Edouard Michelin who, after taking control of their family's rubber and tire business, printed a tourist guidebook for anyone wanting to explore

---

44 *Sawhney, M. S. (2016). Putting products into services. Harvard Business Review, 94(9) 82.*

their home country of France. The book gave tourists all they needed to know to enjoy a long road trip—information on gas stations, hotels, restaurants, and roadside attractions, along with various maps and driving tips. They charged nothing for the first edition of the guidebook, giving away about 35,000 copies. The brothers also started to shift the family business from rubber production to rubber product creations, namely tires. Today, more than a hundred years later, the Michelin Tire Company is the second-largest tire manufacturer in the world, and more than thirty million MICHELIN Guides have been sold worldwide.

As was covered in Chapter One, you can find complementary product ideas by asking questions such as:

- What do our customers need in order to consume more of our services?

- What are customers consuming along with our services?

- How do our customers manage improvements or maintenance?

Since it typically involves leveraging current assets and customers, developing service adjacent products is often a low-risk way to innovate. The urgent and expensive problems still need to be considered, but that is accomplished in a way that complements core service offerings.

Gather Inspiration from Other Solutions

The solution to our customers' urgent and expensive problems may be right in front of us—if we take the time to look. A design sprint is a unique exercise for quickly solving customers' urgent and expensive problems through ideation, prototyping, and testing. My favorite one involves each participant identifying three to five products or services that address some aspect of the urgent and expensive customer problem. They bring screenshots or drawings of each idea to share with the larger group and explain how its features could address the larger problem. Here are some inspirational ideas that were shared during a session for a potential educational technology (EdTech) product designed to help students with learning differences feel more connected:

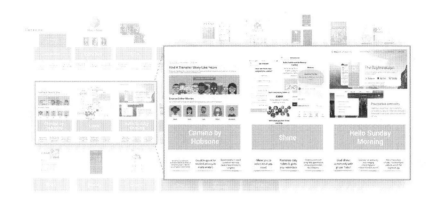

Among this list, only Camino is an EdTech product. However, the other products all have attributes that connect individuals to one another and create a sense of community. These products offered us inspiration in terms of how we could help students with learning differences feel integrated as opposed to left out.

In addition to an exercise like this, it's also a good idea to talk to companies in adjacent spaces to hear what they are doing or considering—and not just the obvious competitors. Talk to start-ups and smaller vendors who tend to be better at innovation. In that vein, you should keep an eye on emerging start-ups in your sector who are using tools such as CB Insights or Crunchbase and plugging into local accelerators and innovation hubs.

Lastly, enlist employees by tapping into their knowledge about customers and competitors. Even if they're not naturally gifted at recognizing patterns or envisioning, they can describe customer needs and are familiar with the other players in the market. Plus, it's a good way to let employees know that we actually want their input—a valuable commodity that they may be holding back. A recent SHRM poll found that 38 percent of employees lacked initiative because they felt that their leaders weren't open to hearing their ideas or dismissed them too quickly. Obtaining employee feedback leads to building a better product; it also improves employee engagement and job satisfaction.

I encourage the organizations to create a volunteer team of junior employees to be champions for innovation, creativity, and applications of new technology. As an example, one company created a grassroots "Team Innovation" whose job was to:

- promote a culture of innovation
- champion new business processes, new business models, new insights, new technologies, new media, new products, and services
- showcase new technologies to elevate knowledge and spark bold thinking
- encourage cross-company collaboration to generate ideas
- look for opportunities for process and productivity improvement

This energetic group hosted outside speakers, took "field trips" to visit other companies, and managed the company's innovation ideas process, whereby new ideas would be screened and selected for pilots.

Often, we need a long list of ideas, both good and bad, to find the next big breakthrough. We might find them using one of the creative exercises above, but we might also use one or two other tricks. Try SCAMPER, for example. SCAMPER was developed by Bob Eberle, education administrator and author, to solve problems or ignite creativity. It's an acronym for seven different types of questions to ask when generating new product ideas:

S – Substitute (What can I substitute to make this product better?)

C – Combine (What ideas, features, processes, people, products, or components can I combine?)

A – Adapt (Which ideas could I adapt, copy, or borrow from other people's products?)

M – Modify (What can I tone down or delete?)

P – Put to another use (What else can it be used for?)

E – Eliminate (What would happen if I removed a component or part of it?)

R – Reverse (What would I do if part of the problem, product, or process worked in reverse?)

Once we have identified top new product ideas, it's time to move on to the next step.

Step 3: Quickly testing concepts with customers and prospects

At this stage, ideas are made tangible by building prototypes and gathering feedback, as well as iterating to refine. My favorite three ways to test new product ideas include concept testing interviews or surveys, co-creation advisory boards, and pre-development MVPs.

Concept Testing Tactic 1: Interviews or Surveys

Just as we tested hypotheses about the customer problem, feedback needs to be gathered through interviews or surveys regarding the best solution. The same tips and strategies apply, only this time, questions will be directed at specific, honest feedback about the product idea, its potential features, target customers' willingness to buy the product, and pricing. Common concept testing questions include:

- How important or relevant is the problem or challenge identified in this idea?

- What stands out the most about this idea?

- How important are each of the following features?

- How often do you see yourself using or interacting with this product?

- What problems or challenges does this product solve for you?

- How likely are you to purchase/invest in this product?

Concept testing can also be a good time to have customers make forced trade-offs between different features being considered. One of my preferred exercises involves allocating "100 pennies" across a set of features to see which ones are the most and least important to different types of buyers and users.

Take the opportunity at this stage to begin testing pricing, packaging, and messaging. Trying to assess how much a buyer is willing to pay can be difficult. Cindy Alvarez, author of *Lean Customer Development,* offers this advice: "Whatever amount people say they will pay for a product that solves their problem is wrong, so don't ask. Instead, ask what they pay for something they already use that provides a similar amount of value or use with the same frequency."

You need not test many potential users; typically, a dozen concept testing interviews are enough. There are times when more is called for, specifically when there are highly distinct buyer and user groups, such as HR executives, hiring managers, and front-line employees. In this case, canvassing five to six buyers or users from each category is recommended.

If the product under review has a user interface (e.g., portal, dashboard, etc.), then this is a good time to get a User Experience (UX) expert involved to develop mock-ups (i.e., wireframes of what the product could look like). If you are not familiar with UX design, it's the simple idea that products should be designed around the user's experience. The importance of good design is illustrated by design pioneer, Alan Cooper. "In Mary Shelley's famous science-fiction novel, *Frankenstein,* the mad Doctor Frankenstein builds a creature from the disparate pieces of dead humans and brings the creature to life with the then-new technology of electricity. Of course, we know this is not actually possible. You cannot create life by sewing together random body parts."[45] The lesson here is that thoughtful design helps to avoid the Frankenstein syndrome.

When hiring UX designers, find someone with a strong mix of skill and experience in graphics, technology, and psychology. It's also important that designers have a thick skin to withstand the feedback.

You may have a very clear picture of how your product will work, but it's important to remember that it will be used by actual people, so you must take into account how they will interact with the product. No matter how well the product solves our customer's problem, it won't be

45 Patton, J., and Economy, P. (2014). *User Story Mapping: Discover the Whole Story, Build the Right Product.* O'Reilly Media, Inc..

successful if they can't figure out how to use it, or don't find it appealing enough to give it a shot. That's why utilizing a good designer is critical in this phase. Design efforts will never be wasted: when it's finally time to bring in a developer, wireframes and user journeys will typically be requested before they start building.

Concept Testing Tactic 2: Co-Creation Advisory Boards

As mentioned in Chapter One, LEGO has been a pioneer in the use of co-creation. The company enlists the help of customers through the LEGO Ideas portal. It's an online community where fans and LEGO creators come together to suggest, iterate, and evaluate ideas for new LEGO kits. Some pretty amazing products have come from the Ideas portal, such as *Women of NASA*, *The Beatles' Yellow Submarine*, the *DeLorean* from *Back to the Future*, and the motel from *Schitt's Creek*.

The process is simple. Customers log into the portal to submit an idea for a new kit; then, the over 875,000 people who are "members" of the Ideas portal vote on the kits they want to see come to life. It takes 10,000 votes for an idea to move forward. While that's no easy feat, LEGO Ideas typically reduced marketing time for new kits from 2 years to 6 months. Every single kit developed from this approach has been a bestseller, with 90 percent of kits selling out in their first release.

The beauty of co-creation is that it keeps the customer at the center of new product development. As I've mentioned previously, the biggest mistake I see companies make when developing new products is not developing a product that solves an urgent and expensive customer problem. Co-creation systems can help to avoid this mistake.

One of my favorite co-creation approaches is one learned early in my career. It's a "charter advisor" model where select customers and prospects are invited to help articulate the problem to be solved and the solution to be developed. As with LEGO, the result has been a quicker path to marketing products that both solve real problems and delight customers.

Two flavors of the charter advisor co-creation model are discussed below.

Co-Creation Charter Advisory Board Model 1: Co-Fund the Development

In this model, customers agree to help direct and fund product development in exchange for a beta customer license for the first year and favorable pricing thereafter. Since the product will be designed with their input and testing, it's a safe bet that it will meet their needs.

Advantages:

- Your business gets help with funding product development.

- The process attracts only the most serious customers.

- There's more commitment to the development process because of the "skin in the game."

Disadvantages:

- As you are essentially pre-selling the product, there's a longer initial recruitment cycle.

- The process typically requires a brand that is already strong, a loyal customer base, or social proof.

- You may forego some early revenue because advisors receive discounted pricing.

Co-Creation Charter Advisory Board Model 2: Advise, Then Buy

Similar to other groups I've discussed previously, customers and prospects in this model are invited to join a select advisory group, to advise on product design with the opportunity to purchase a beta license (or receive a free beta license) and then purchase post beta.

Advantages:

- It's easier to recruit advisors and initial customers because the request is for time, not money.

- This model is good for start-ups or new to the market as it can help overcome lack of brand recognition and/or a strong customer base, as well as social proof.

Disadvantages:

- The process requires more up-front capital.

- The advisors may be less committed to the process or the product because they don't have "skin in the game."

Whichever way you structure the co-creation approach, the charter advisors receive early access to the product and contribute heavily to its design. The approach for recruiting co-creators is essentially the same for both models: start with an invitation-only, exclusive offer to be part of a group of charter advisors to design the product. Begin by targeting well-known industry thought-leaders; once they are on board, it is much easier to recruit the rest. Strive to recruit a mix of existing customers and prospects to help ensure that the product's design will attract new customers.

Typically, at least one pitch or prewire conversation with each invitee is needed to secure their interest in co-creating. Keep in mind that it usually takes more than one conversation if you're also asking for an upfront development contribution, as in model number one above. The primary value proposition for being a charter advisor is the ability to help design the product. Serving as a charter advisor also gives the invitees the ability to network and benchmark with other advisors, and they are able to enjoy other optional features such as exclusive access before competitors, access to market analytics, or insights generated during the product development process, as well as discounts after the product is launched.

Once a critical mass of advisors has been recruited (at least a dozen), the next step is to convene the group of charter advisors to discuss design questions. This works well as one half-day session, or across several sessions, including an initial meet and greet to plan the first development sprint, followed by two or three more sprint demo sessions.

Once the advisory group has been recruited, there are some important tasks to complete to ensure success. In preparation for the first session, collect and share the bios of all members, as each member will want to know who else is involved. Also, communicate a clear agenda in advance (along with the list of attendees) to promote attendance and engagement.

During the first session, the key goals are to:

- Clearly understand the main problems or challenges facing advisors

- Solicit specific feedback on the product and the features being considered (try a forced trade-off exercise during the session, or as a pre-meeting survey. The 100 pennies exercise previously mentioned would work well here.)

- Collect input on price points and willingness to pay

One company I worked with used co-creation to make a better, data-driven way to predict and manage risk in the food supply chain. They convened a group of 14 leading supply chain, risk, sourcing, and food safety executives drawn from some of the largest and most innovative food companies around the world. The value proposition was giving customers (or prospects) the opportunity to meet and learn from each other, have a hand in creating a product that solves an important problem, and enjoy early access and category exclusivity to the product. The process and the extent of their commitment were clearly outlined in advance (a total of 5 sessions—4 with their peers and one 1:1 interview) so that everyone knew what to expect.

As Photonic founder and CEO Dr. Tony Atti described it, "Co-creation is about helping the customer imagine a different future." The real kicker is that it's a future they help to create.

 CHARTER CUSTOMER ADVISORY BOARD TOOLKIT
(visit *www.theproductizebook.com* to download the tools.)

Concept Testing Tactic 3: Pre-development MVPs

Since people aren't good at imagining their own responses in hypothetical situations, you must go beyond asking questions and running live tests in order to thoroughly vet a product concept. During an interview, people may say that they'd be willing to buy a certain product, but will they follow through? Hypotheses must therefore be tested in the market as opposed to relying on customer feedback.

There is a range of fast and thorough techniques for market testing, but I prefer "pre-development" Minimum Viable Products. (MVPs were covered in detail in Chapter One.) In particular, three types of pre-development MVPs are recommended: Sell-then-build, Wizard of Oz, and Concierge Testing.

Sell-then-build

"Sell-then-build" is aptly named. Sell the product concept first; then, if there is enough interest, the actual product is built. For higher-priced products, the product can be sold as a "pilot" or consulting-type project to a few key customers who help fund the development. For lower-priced products that may be purchased online, a sell-then-build approach would involve advertising or email marketing to direct potential customers and leading them to a product "landing page." On the landing page, potential buyers provide their email addresses in order to learn more, schedule a sales conversation, or even pre-purchase the product (depending on the product and the price point). This system allows for testing the market's appetite for the product (as measured by click-throughs, sign-ups, etc.) as well as testing different value propositions, product features, and target segments.

Sell-then-build is the idea behind Kickstarter, with which you are likely familiar. It's a platform for sell-then-build products that uses a landing page describing a product and inviting customers to buy before the products are made. Product ideas range from world-changing to downright wacky. One woman raised over $1400, 3 times her goal, to create 100 little birds out of wire and felt. Who knew that there was a market for wire and felt birds? This woman did, and she learned it without first spending a dime on wire or felt.

Using an official sell-then-build platform like Kickstarter to test our MVP isn't the only path: a landing page on your company website will do. The landing page needs to explain the product's features and the problem it will solve for customers. Depending on the product, the landing page can entice people to pay in advance, or their names can be added to a waitlist ensuring that they're among the product's first buyers.

The goal is to measure genuine demand for the product. This usually comes in the form of people signing up for our waitlist or giving us money in advance. We can also collect feedback from a short survey about why they are interested in the product and the features that are most important.

Wizard of Oz Testing

Toto was the real hero of the *Wizard of Oz* when he pulled back the curtain to reveal that the giant talking wizard head was just a sweet old man appearing all-powerful. The wizard wasn't trying to pull off a nefarious deception. His intentions were honorable; he just didn't have the skills yet to be good at his job. Wizard of Oz prototyping is similar in that it gives the impression that a product idea is fully-functioning and automated when in actuality, it's under development. There is work being done in the background, but customers don't need to know that it's happening.

You needn't worry that Wizard of Oz prototyping is a nefarious deception; rather, it's a manual simulation of what a real product could look like and do. It's a way to avoid building expensive systems or platforms until the real demand for a product or solution is ascertained. And since testing is performed manually, quick modifications can be made to the product, allowing for rapid testing of many hypotheses in search of the most effective solution.

Zappos shoe company was initiated using Wizard of Oz prototyping. Nick Swinmurn came up with the idea of selling shoes online while struggling to find a desirable pair of boots. The idea struck him when he was at a shoe store in the mall. In an interview with Fortune, Nick says he approached the store manager and said, "I'll take some pictures, put your shoes online, and if people buy them, I'll buy them from you at full price." And so he set up an online store. When people ordered shoes, he'd go to the store, buy the shoes, and ship them to the customer. He was the man behind the curtain until he no longer needed to be. Now, consumers can hop onto Zappos.com to purchase any shoe desired; within two days, the merchandise arrives at their home.

The Concierge Test

The Concierge Test is similar to Wizard of Oz prototyping in that the work is still done manually, but in this case, customers know it's happening. Concierge testing lets us try out our product idea by first providing it to a small group in beta form.

A commonly shared example of good concierge testing is the development story behind Rent the Runway. If you aren't familiar, Rent the Runway is an online platform enabling people to rent designer clothing and jewelry at a fraction of the retail ownership cost. The women behind the now $100 million company started with two beta tests. The first test offered college students a chance to come in, try on clothes to rent, and then return the items. It was a success. So, they moved to the second test, which allowed women to see the clothes, and to rent them, but without the ability to try them on. Women still participated. With two successful betas under their belts, the founders knew they had an idea that was ready for scale.

Manually working out what the product will be and how customers engage with it is a high touch form of testing. While it is manually intensive, concierge testing provides rich insight into our customers' needs and desires because we're right there with them. Eventually, products can be scaled up and some (or all) of the human touch can be removed.

Regardless of the chosen testing method, the goal is to see how real customers engage authentically. Testing allows for quick and easy evolution of the product concept. By learning about customers' needs and wants, your product can avoid becoming the next Satisfries.

Step 4: Developing preliminary business models and modeling revenue and profit potential to make a Go/No-Go decision

In this phase, a preliminary business model of the revenue and profit potential of your product idea is developed. This helps in making a "Go" or "No-Go" decision before proceeding with the more expensive product development step.

It's important to remember that any business model created at this stage is just a hypothesis. Assumptions around the market size of our target segments, market penetration, price, and costs (or effort) should be updated at each stage in the pathway. For each new product idea, a hypothesis should be created regarding:

- Volume: How many customers can we gain/retain with this new idea?

- Price: What sort of price point or price improvement can we expect?

- Confidence: How confident are we in terms of successful production and marketing?

- Effort: How much energy and/or resources will the launch of a successful product require?

At this stage, it's also important to start discussing whether to Build, Buy, or Partner to develop the idea.

- **Build** in-house (or with outsourced developers) which requires expertise to manage the development resources.

- **Buy** via an acquisition that requires the most up-front investment, but also reduces development risk (and if already in-market, the risk of not having product-market fit.)

- **Partner** with a co-creator for development, as Jim Price at Empower did when he partnered with ad tech startup Martin to build the ClearTrade programmatic media platform. To make a partnership like this work, a revenue share agreement is formed which lowers the lifetime value of the investment, but it also reduces the amount of up-front capital required and lowers the risk of mismanagement if we do not have the capabilities up front. Licensing of part of the technology required can also be considered. Again, licensing lowers up-front investment and reduces mismanagement risk, but it brings the downside of relinquishing control over some of the underlying intellectual property.

Another example mentioned in the Introduction is Accenture's AIP+ service, which provides Accenture's clients with access to AI tools and applications from a network of partner vendors. By partnering with technology vendors, Accenture does not have to invest in the engineering resources to develop those technologies in-house. Similarly, Accenture's technology partners gain access to new clients and markets without having to sell the services themselves.[46]

---

46 *CB Insights. (October 8, 2020). Killing Strategy: The Disruption of Management Consulting.*

Yet another example is Bain's Net Promoter Score (NPS) Prism, a product that was launched in collaboration with the SaaS survey business Qualtrics. The product takes the NPS intellectual property that Bain created and gives client companies a quick and easy way to collect and compare the NPS of different internal teams, products and markets, and other companies in their industry. This is all done through the Qualtrics SaaS tools and dashboard, a component that Bain did not have to build.[47]

To make a Go/No-Go decision, pull together the following information and review it with your leadership team or product advisory board.

- Exactly what problem will this solve? (value proposition)
- For whom do we solve that problem? (target market)
- How big is the opportunity? (market size)
- What alternatives are out there? (competitive landscape)
- Why are we best suited to pursue this? (our differentiator)
- Why now? (market window)
- How will we get this product to market? (go-to-market strategy)
- How will we measure success/make money from this product? (metrics/revenue strategy)
- What factors are critical to success? (solution requirements)
- Given the above, what's the recommendation? (go or no-go?)

---

47 CB Insights. (October 8, 2020). *Killing Strategy: The Disruption of Management Consulting.*

Step 5: Translating market requirements into stories and product requirements

Once you have a concept for a product that solves customers' urgent and expensive problems and you've moved into development, you'll need designers and developers to build a functioning product that delights users.

If you haven't had a lead developer and designer working with you up to this point, you will need to explain to her or him what you've learned about the market's needs, as well as the longer-term vision for the product and any untested hypotheses. In other words, you cannot just hand the developer and designer a list of product requirements. Co-design and development aren't just about seeing customers as partners, these steps are also about seeing developers as partners.

If you haven't already done so, share the product strategy document that was created to make the Go/No-Go decision with developers and designers. Since this document outlines the vision for the product (i.e., the value proposition), target customers (i.e., personas), the customer problem the product solves, and the objectives/key results, it's a key piece of the puzzle.

You'll also need to outline the desired product features, the customer problem each feature solves, and the priority for the feature (i.e., include in the first iteration, next iteration, longer-term iteration). Note that the list of features is a flexible list that will evolve over time.

 PRODUCT STRATEGY TEMPLATE FOR DEVELOPERS
(visit *www.theproductizebook.com* to download the tools.)

Step 6: Working with developers to build a functioning front-end and back-end

Will you hire in-house developers or will you contract development out? Unless you already have in-house developers, it's usually a good idea to use contract developers initially. Brian Joseph at RevJen admits he had zero experience developing products, so he used his network to find people who did. Jim Price's team at Empower created partnerships with organizations possessing the talent he needed. Hiring developers to come in-house offers more control and lowers our overall costs. Conversely, outsourced support is flexible and quick to bring onboard.

If you decide to contract, here are some questions from MojoTech[48] to ask when hiring or contracting developers:

- Can I see what you're doing on my project on a daily or weekly basis?

- Can I adjust my feature set and specifications as we go?

- Can I meet and work directly with the designers and developers on my project?

- Who owns the code and designs you produce for me (i.e., the work product and deliverables)? *Note: Make sure you own the code and work product!*

- Will you help me transition to an in-house team, or mentor and train my team?

It's important to remember that when building and launching, the chosen resource model may be suboptimal in the short-term in exchange for more

---

48 Kishfy, N. (2012). 5 Non-Technical Questions To Ask When Hiring A Development Firm. MojoTech.

flexibility. Even if you do contract out, you'll still need the infrastructure to find and manage a vendor or team of contractors.

When working with developers, either in-house or outsourced, here are a few helpful tips:

- Learn the basics. Working with developers of tech-enabled products can sometimes feel like conversing with someone who speaks a different language because developers do, in some respects, speak their own language. To make the most of their technical skills and expertise, you'll need to learn some basic concepts. For example, there is front-end or "client-side" development—this is everything the user sees and interacts with and also where the UX designer's skills come into play. Additionally, there's the back-end or "server-side" development which focuses on the product's functionality.

- Always ask how much development time a new feature will take to create before seriously considering adding it to your product.

- Invite developers to co-create the design (not just execute it) by letting them know what customer problem the potential new feature is supposed to solve and asking if they have a better feature idea for that problem. Also, ask how product design can be maintained as simply as possible. For example: Where could third-party software be used versus custom development?[49]

- Remember that development tends to take longer than expected. In some ways, it can be a lot like remodeling a house: be prepared for it to take longer and cost more than what you have estimated.

---

49 Garber, S. (March 14, 2013). 5 Best Practices for Working with Developers. Forbes.

Step 7: Continuously soliciting user feedback

Throughout the product's development, testing and learning must be ongoing. Do you feel like you're listening to a broken record? This point has been driven home so many times because checking in with customers is vital. The importance of ensuring that customers' needs are met, that the product is functioning properly, and that it's easy for them to understand and use cannot be overstated.

Beginning the process with some understanding of the subtle yet important differences between the two categories of testing (user testing and usability testing) is useful. Here's a simple explanation from UXBlog: "User Testing is about 'Will this user use my product?' where usability testing is to figure out 'Can this user use this product?'"[50]

Both user and usability testing helps to collect deep information about customers' experiences in using your product. But the goals are different. The primary goal of user testing is to learn more about customer behavior, preferences, and opinions so that their requirements are continually met. User testing consists of having customers evaluate the product by going through an early version project or prototype to identify if and how it meets their needs. The primary goal of usability testing is to identify problems or bugs in the design. Customers should actually use the product so that you can understand and improve their experience with it. Both user and usability testing share the goal of trying to find opportunities to improve the product for the next iteration.

Neither form of testing requires a big sample of participants; three to five customers are usually enough. In fact, Jakob Nielsen, PhD, principal of the Nielsen Norman Group, argues that any more than that is a waste of

---

50 Mishra, V. (2016). User Testing v/s Usability Testing. theuxblog.com

time and money. "As you add more and more users, you learn less and less because you will keep seeing the same things again and again. There is no real need to keep observing the same thing multiple times, and you will be very motivated to go back to the drawing board and redesign the site to eliminate the usability problems."[51]

In order to gain insight from each of the users for whom the product has been designed, it's preferable that testers represent target personas. Most user testing generates in-depth qualitative feedback, so having only a few participants helps to keep both cost and timeline under control. It's also crucial that testing involves the customer actually using the product or prototype; that way, the feedback is authentic as opposed to theoretical (i.e., *show me how you use this product* versus *explain how you would use this product*). User and usability testing may be done at the same time and can take on a number of different forms.

- **Individual in-depth interviews** – A trained test moderator runs a test with the help of a prepared script and task scenarios, then gathers feedback from the user on the experience.

- **Focus groups** – A trained test moderator facilitates a discussion between small groups of users.

- **A/B testing** – Users are given two versions of a digital product in order to determine which one performs better.

- **Heat maps** – The user's mouse tracking is evaluated to see how she or he interacts with the product.

- **Observation** – Users are observed as they perform certain functions integral to the product.

---

51 Nielsen, J. (2000). *Why You Only Need to Test with 5 Users. Nielsen Norman Group.*

Whichever form of testing you choose, stick to the customer rules outlined previously: be clear as to what you want to learn, ask open-ended questions, and adjust hypotheses to reflect your learning. Last, but not least, don't forget that every iteration of a product requires more testing.

Action Steps

1. Identify existing assets that you have that could be transformed into a product to meet your customers' urgent and expensive customer problems. Where do you have *unique* intellectual property? What data have you collected as part of your existing services? What processes have you documented as part of our existing services that you could codify?

2. Consider bringing together a group of existing customers or prospects to provide feedback on concepts or prototypes? Who should be included? What sorts of varying perspectives do you need? Outline the next steps to convene your first group.

3. Compare and contrast buy, build, and partner options for your most attractive product ideas. Be honest about your capabilities with each. Do you have the skills in-house? Are those skilled people already fully devoted to client work? How could you free them up? Do you have the cash or equity to buy the skills or bring in an outsourced provider? What do you have to offer potential partners in exchange for access to their talent?

PART THREE
BE FEARLESS

"It is not the critic who counts; not the man who points out how the strong man stumbles, or where the doer of deeds could have done them better. The credit belongs to the man who is actually in the arena, whose face is marred by dust and sweat and blood; who strives valiantly; who errs, who comes short again and again, because there is no effort without error and shortcoming; but who does actually strive to do the deeds; who knows great enthusiasms, the great devotions; who spends himself in a worthy cause; who at the best knows in the end the triumph of high achievement, and who at the worst, if he fails, at least fails while daring greatly, so that his place shall never be with those cold and timid souls who neither know victory nor defeat."

- Citizenship in a Republic by Theodore Roosevelt

The Productize Pathway

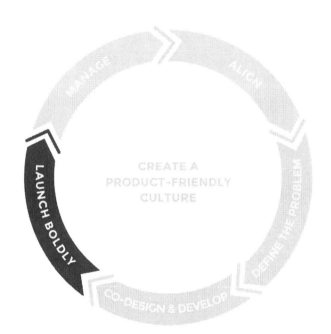

Chapter Seven

MISTAKE: Fear of Cannibalization Hinders Sales and Marketing
SOLUTION: Launch Boldly

At Vecteris, we give a framed copy of Theodore Roosevelt's 'Daring Greatly' quote to all new employees. It's a celebration of fearlessness, one of our core values and an essential ingredient for successful innovation.

In the **Launch Boldly** phase, planning occurs as to how new products will be marketed to existing customers and how they will attract new customers. Equally important is planning how to drive new customers to our existing services, and mapping how customers may go from products to services and back to products.

There are five parts to Launching Boldly:

- Address our biggest fear: cannibalization

- Develop pricing strategies and packages

- Create messaging to articulate the value proposition to target different segments

- Create a multi-channel marketing plan
- Develop a sales strategy and win the hearts and minds of the sales team

Addressing these areas will ensure a strong go-to-market strategy. Let's start with tackling cannibalization fears that you or your team may be experiencing.

Cannibalization Fears Kill Good Products

Fear of cannibalizing current services or products can kill our best products before they even have a chance to succeed. Total or partial cannibalization can occur when a new product moves customers away from current service offerings or product lines. Many executives get caught up in the fear that new products will detract—or worse, destroy—their existing business, which is why I call this phase **Launch Boldly** as opposed to "launch." If you are to be successful, you must address any cannibalization fears and move past them.

To help, I've developed a simple framework to use when examining and addressing cannibalization fears. I call it the 3 C's of Cannibalization: Customers, Complementary, Christensen.

Customers: Successful products all start with clear customer needs and target customer segments.

To mitigate the impact of cannibalization (notice I did not say "eliminate"—more on that later), start by clearly defining the customers using your _current_ services or products. As I discussed in Chapter Five, customer personas can be created for the people who are actually using our product. These personas describe consumers' demographics, goals, fears, and values, and describe the problems that our product or service solves for each customer segment.

It is recommended that you go through the same process for the *new product* that you are considering.

- Which customers will be interested in this new product?
- What are the characteristics or personas of each target customer segment?
- What problems will this new product solve for each segment?

Next, perform a side-by-side comparison of the personas and problems of *current* customer segments with the *new* customer segments to see how much overlap exists. If most of the attributes overlap, your new product may cannibalize part of your existing revenue. If the circles are mutually exclusive, then the new product is unlikely to cannibalize. For example, if you are creating a feature-light product offered at a lower price point to attract a more cost-conscious customer, there likely won't be much overlap between the customer segments. Let's revisit Empower's MediaAgent product to illustrate this. MediaAgent is a SaaS planning tool for smaller companies who cannot afford, or need, the more bespoke media planning work Empower does for large clients. MediaAgent uses data to help companies plan and buy advertising across television, radio, and digital platforms. There is little concern about cannibalization because MediaAgent is geared toward smaller clients who need less support and who aren't willing to pay as much.

Complementary: Find a product that is a good partner for our existing services.

According to David Robertson, author of _The Power of Little Ideas: A Low-Risk, High-Reward Approach to Innovation_, one way to avoid canni-balization is to focus on developing complementary innovations around our current services. I love this idea because not only does it generate new revenue, but it also enhances our existing services by making them even more appealing and valuable to our customer base. That's why, as Robertson says, it's a low-risk approach, one in which expertise is leveraged and core services strengthened. It's also a high-reward approach because current customers will receive more while the door is opened to attract new customers. "The real trick is to identify complementary products," says Shuba Swaminathan, Partner & Google Cloud Growth Leader at IBM, ". . . that will be taking advantage of our marketing expertise gained from acquiring present customers and our existing customer goodwill."[52]

Christensen: As in Clay Christensen and the pattern of disruption described in his classic book The Innovator's Dilemma.

In _The Innovator's Dilemma_, the late Clayton Christensen explains that companies can do everything "right" but still fail when new, unexpected competitors rise and take over the market. Christensen refers to these competitors as disruptors, and the concept of their market takeover as disruptive innovation. "Disruptive Innovation describes a process by which a product or service initially takes root in simple applications at the bottom of a market—typically by being less expensive and more accessible—and then relentlessly moves upmarket, eventually displacing

---

52 _Shuba Swaminathan, 3 Steps to Keep Your New Product From Cannibalizing Your Existing Product, from Inc.com originally on Quora_

established competitors."[53] The dilemma is that established companies tend to protect what they have and run away from products that might cannibalize. Now, with more disruptive threats on the horizon than in the past, businesses willing to cannibalize existing revenue streams are more likely to survive.

Consider this advice from Scott Anthony, co-author of *Dual Transformation: How to Reposition Today's Business While Creating the Future*: ". . . companies must come to grips with their cannibalization concerns because getting overly defensive can curtail powerful growth strategies." Self-cannibalism can renew a firm's competitive advantage and introduce a previously unthought of value proposition. The most common and notable example of successful self-cannibalism is Apple's iPhone, which immediately made the iPod series obsolete. In retrospect, it would be hard to argue that cannibalization wasn't a smart move on Apple's part.

Be prepared to think like a competitor, even if it means plotting a course that may eventually put you out of an existing line of business. Also, be aware that leveraging the 3 C's of cannibalization requires research! The most important part of mitigating the negative effects of cannibalization is undertaking the correct market research and analysis upfront. You'll need to analyze current usage behaviors, talk to customers and prospects, and understand the competitive landscape. Will your target customer segments be attracted to your new product? A few small tests are recommended to see if your hypotheses in this important area are correct. The same tools discussed in Chapter Five around defining the problem can be utilized for this purpose.

New products should either meet the needs of new customer segments, work in partnership with our current products or services, or play into the

---

53 *(n.d.) Disruptive Innovation. Christensen Institute. Online.*

idea that we are stealing business from ourselves before our competitors do. In the Launch Boldly phase, packaging and pricing of new products can be done in a way that augments and creates demand for existing services without the need to fully protect those services.

Developing Pricing Strategies and Packages to Target Different Segments

To ready a product for the market, its features, price points, and packages should be designed to meet customer needs across a variety of customer segments. I encourage clients to use a multi-tiered pricing strategy such as Good, Better, Best, or Bronze, Silver, Gold (or some variation of those levels). Pricing is based on a quality threshold with the "good" level reflecting the bare bones of the product features, "better" encompassing all the features of the basic model plus a few advanced ones, and the "best" means being fully loaded with all the bells and whistles.

Rafi Mohammed, founder of Culture of Profit, points out that tiered pricing is quite common and helps companies attract price-conscious customers while also giving less price-conscious customers the opportunity to spend more. He says, "In the modern era, G-B-B pricing is evident in many product categories. Gas stations sell regular, plus, and super fuel. American Express offers a range of credit cards, including green, gold, platinum, and black, with varying benefits and annual fees. Cable TV providers market basic, extended, and premium packages. Car washes typically offer several options, separated by services such as waxing and undercoating."[54]

---

54 Mohammed, R. (2018). *The Good Better Best Approach to Pricing. Harvard Business Review, 96(5), 106-115.*

To create tiered pricing bundles, we need to choose the attributes to add, drop, or vary to create different perceptions of value. Common attributes include volume (low, medium, unlimited), level of service, features, flexibility, and wait time.

Another pricing strategy is to have both free and paid versions of the products—commonly referred to as "Freemium." As the name suggests, this strategy combines "free" and "premium." Take a product like TurboTax: many users can use the free version because their tax needs are straightforward and they file a 1040EZ; however, someone who works as a freelancer or who owns rental properties will likely opt for the paid version because their tax situation is more complicated. Users opting for the free product are given limited features while premium users have access to a greater range of product features.

"Freemium" models are prolific, including such examples as LinkedIn, cloud storage, and TV channel streaming. But there are B2B versions as well. My team uses Zapier to connect many of our digital tools. When we first started out, we used the free option because we only needed to connect a few accounts. When our business and digital tool usage grew, we upgraded to the paid account. That's the essence of the Freemium model: it gives customers little to no barrier to accessing a limited version of the product, sells them on its value by letting them try it, and then upgrades them to a paid version that meets their needs even better.

Anil Prahlad, Chief Content Officer at Hanover Research, believes organizations need to be willing to experiment with Freemium. Hanover provides custom research and analytics for the business, education, and healthcare sectors. Hanover offers quality, free content to get people in, and then eventually charges for deeper analysis. "We did this with toolkits and lesson plans that teachers can download from our website after giving us their email," says Anil. The free content offers enough value to entice customers to want to pay for more.

Options needn't be limited to two choices; for example, it's possible to have a free, premium, and pro version. Pricing a product this way doesn't just lower the customer entry barrier, it also acts as a market test of our product. If the top-tiered package isn't selling, it's either priced too high or customers aren't seeing the added value. And if the lowest-tiered package isn't selling, it may mean that higher packages are priced too low.

It's a mistake to initially price a product on the low side just because it's an immature product. Although a premium price shouldn't be charged on a very immature product, we also don't want to anchor the beginning price too low as it will hurt our ability to charge more in the future. Be very clear that lower, introductory pricing is introductory. Market a version of the product that is priced competitively enough to engage customers, but at a level that also reflects the value provided by the product. Consider implementing a lower "introductory" or first year pricing (while piloting the product on a limited basis) and then upping prices in year two.

The other decision to make when determining the pricing of a product is whether to price based on the number of users, tiers of the number of users, or enterprise pricing. Most organizations also need to think about pricing per product or pricing based on "all access." If you're launching a product that already has industry standards for units of measurement, it's best to stick with that structure so that buyers will already be familiar with the comparative pricing scheme.

Messaging that Articulates the Value Proposition

The most effective messaging focuses on the product of the product's product. Yes, you read that right. The most effective ad campaigns market an item that is two or three steps removed from the actual product. Imagine that you want to sell perfume or cologne . . . The product is a fragrant, yellow liquid, but why does anyone want a fragrant, yellow liquid? People enjoy smelling nice, that's why. So, the end goal of the product (or the product's product) is secondary to the perfume itself. But why does someone want to smell nice? The answer is because they want to feel attractive in the eyes of others, making that state of being the product of the product's product. When thinking about every perfume or cologne ad that's ever been made, the commodity being sold isn't just the perfume; it's the hope that the product will make oneself attractive to others. The end goal is several steps removed from the start line.

I'll offer my own company as a good B2B example. At Vecteris, we conduct research and make recommendations (our product) in order to help organizations innovate and successfully launch new products (our product's product). The new products help our clients scale and create recurring revenue with a higher margin. So, our product's product's product is a way to scale services and generate recurring, high-margin revenue.

Once you've uncovered the essence of a product, messaging needs to be developed to market it. That messaging should include:

- A lead message for the product that embodies its essence. In other words, describe what it does and the benefit(s) of it (e.g., "we help you innovate more effectively to scale services and generate recurring, high-margin revenue").

- Secondary messages for each persona that speak to their unique needs (e.g., "for large teams, we help you develop a common innovation process and playbook").

- Urgency drivers for purchasing the product. Why should customers buy this now versus waiting a year? (e.g., "Most consulting firms are facing significant disruption from digital-first competitors who have better data and are lower cost.")

- Differentiators for the product. What makes our product more effective than existing solutions? (e.g., "Unlike other solutions providers, we have deep expertise in helping professional services firms innovate to create more scalable, tech-enabled products and services.")

In his book *Crossing the Chasm: Marketing and Selling High-Tech Products to Mainstream Customers*, Geoffrey Moore offers a good template for messaging. He suggests outlining an elevator pitch for a product idea:

- For (target customers)

- Who are dissatisfied with (the current market alternative)

- Our product is a (new product category)

- That provides (key problem-solving capability and benefits—this is where we mention the product's product's product)

- Unlike . . . (insert product alternative), our product . . . (insert key product features).

The final component of effective messaging includes using case studies, ideally told as stories. Storytelling is powerful: it's a medium that calls people to action and allows them to connect. Paul Zak, Founding Director of the Center for Neuroeconomics Studies, wrote a *Harvard Business*

Review article a few years ago discussing a study that showed how good storytelling "hacks" the oxytocin system to motivate people to engage in certain behaviors.[55] This oxytocin "hack" can be a powerful tool to message the benefits of our product. Zak's advice: "When you want to motivate, persuade, or be remembered, start with a story of human struggle and eventual triumph. It will capture people's hearts—by first attracting their brains."

 POSITIONING STATEMENT (AKA "ELEVATOR PITCH") TEMPLATE
(visit *www.theproductizebook.com* to download the tools.)

Creating a Multi-Channel Marketing Plan

Once you have your messaging, you need to share that message wherever your customers are spending time—for example, business press, email, conferences, LinkedIn, search engines, etc. The most effective strategy involves multi-channel messaging. It's important to keep in mind that multi-channel doesn't mean multi-message. Successful multi-channel strategies are designed around the same customer persona(s) and create consistent experiences across all platforms.

Another part of the multi-channel messaging strategy is thinking about tactics to be used at different phases of the customer journey. For example, marketing tactics will be different at the building awareness phase (e.g., PR, conferences, advertising) than it will be when awareness has been achieved and differentiating our product from the competition is the goal (through webinars, nurture campaigns, etc.).

---

55 Zak, P. (October 28, 2014). *Why Your Brain Loves Good Storytelling. Harvard Business Review: Boston.*

This is also the time to ensure that the company brand supports the new product brand. If, for example, part of your company's brand promise is that you take a very customized approach with each customer, that component will be incongruent with the brand of a more scalable product; therefore, you may need to create a product brand that is separate from the company brand. "You can't keep our old website that just talks about all of our consulting services. It confuses customers right off the bat," says Dejan Duzevik. When he was Chief Product Officer at Concentric, an analytics software firm that began as a consulting firm, Dejan says one of the biggest mistakes they made was waiting until after they had launched products to think about their brand. He said that in his ten years at Concentric, the greatest impact on revenue occurred when they refreshed the company brand to match their new product strategy.

 **Multi-Channel Marketing Campaign Planning Template**
(visit *www.theproductizebook.com* to download the tools.)

Developing a Sales Strategy and Winning the Hearts and Minds of the Sales Team

Selling a customized service and selling a more standardized product are two very different things. Even though an urgent and expensive customer problem has been identified and a great product or solution to meet that need has been developed, if there's no sales channel to effectively sell the new product, it won't be a success. This is a challenging situation because the divide between selling a custom solution and selling a scalable product is a large one. "If you can't cross this divide it doesn't matter what else you do," says, Chief Executive Officer of NaviStone, Larry Kavanaugh.

And the Head of Product for a global consulting firm put it this way: "Going to market and selling are hard, and companies should organize around it earlier. We assumed the consultants and partners would be able to sell our new product because they sell a ton of consulting business and are talking to the right people. But the skills for selling consulting services do not automatically transfer into skills for selling standardized products."

Organizations often need a different sales team or channel to sell products. The economics of a product sale are different (typically lower price point, but higher margin) and rely heavily on lead generation and product demos, sales tools that your consultants and partners may not have experience using.

If your current sales team is to sell the new products, you need to win their hearts and minds. This requires a compelling and transparent explanation of how a strategy of offering standardized products supports your organization's mission and vision. You must explain the commercial relationship between services and products, and clearly communicate the value proposition for existing clients and new customers. These conversations cannot occur just once; they need to happen over and over.

First and foremost, make sure the salesforce knows what they are selling and why it is valuable to customers. This sounds ridiculously obvious, but when a product is developed and launched quickly, it's easy to forget the importance of taking the time to explain the move. Introducing the sales team to the new product and sales process is critical to building trust among the sales team and for giving them the knowledge needed to effectively sell it. They don't need to know the ins and outs, but they do need an overall understanding, including the "why" of the product. What problem is it solving? What is the true market for it? Share the market learnings from the "Define the Problem" phase, as well as buyer and user feedback on the concept.

Secondly, be very clear with your sales team and customers that this is an iterative product development process; the first version is not the final version and the product will evolve as market feedback is received. The main points to keep in mind:

- Clearly communicate the product roadmap to the sales team so they know which new features are coming, and when.

- Explain why you structured the roadmap the way you did, so the sales team knows the customer problem the product solves in its current version, as well as the customer problems to be solved with future versions.

Thirdly, as a way of gathering valuable insights into market needs (and customer reactions), ask for sales feedback during the product innovation process. The opportunity to provide feedback will make the sales team feel more invested in the product and more equipped to sell it.

Next, build a selling toolbox; spend the necessary resources to create good collateral. When developing marketing collateral, it's common to think about the client and forget that marketing collateral also gives the sales team the confidence that investing in all levels of the product launch brings. So, don't skip this step no matter how quickly the product is moving. In addition to the marketing collateral, give your salespeople an arsenal of tools to make their job easy. This includes things like a thirty-second elevator pitch, a sales deck, an FAQ document, a product demo (video or live with a script), objection handling talking points, an overview of how the product is different from what competitors offer, and anything else that someone learning about the new product needs to know, or that you want them to know.

Keep in mind that product demos should be tailored to the customer. Good demos are not rock solid, set-in-stone plans; rather, a good demo acts as a playbook. As Robert Falcone, author and head of Sales Engineering at Guru puts it, "You want to know all the plays but only run the ones you need in the moment."[56]

Last but not least, align sales incentives to encourage selling of the new product. Think back to the commission model Christoffer Ellehuus used at Strategy Execution to encourage the team to sell products over consulting engagements. The sales commission for product sales was *twice* that of consulting sales.

Brian Joseph of RevJen found that he needed a few things to win the hearts and minds of his sales team. First, a compelling vision for how their products were going to help achieve the organization's mission. Second, a good list of beta customers and testimonials. Third, incentives that encouraged selling the most scalable products. Fourth, constant communication about the company, products, and emphasizing the vision. And fifth, clear guidance on the ideal customer lifecycle. In other words, explaining his vision for how a customer would buy one product, and then another, and then potentially, future products or services. Defining the ideal customer lifecycle requires us to define which products are good introductory products and which products should be reserved for add-ons or cross-sell.

It's also important to plan to iterate. Build in a schedule to evaluate the market feedback, marketing tools, sales pitch, etc. with the team and refresh collateral if needed. Ask the sales team what's working, what needs to be revised, and what additional research is needed to better understand the customers or the market landscape. Lastly, someone from the sales

56 First Round Review. (n.d.) Your Product Demo Sucks Because It's Focused on Your Product.

team should also sit on the Product Innovation Board—if you've put one in place. Keeping the conversations flowing to and from the sales team will lead to a better understanding of customer needs; moreover, that back and forth sharing of ideas will also help you to win the hearts of your sales team.

 Go-to-Market Checklist and Templates
(visit *www.theproductizebook.com* to download the tools.)

Action Steps

1. Use the 3Cs framework to address cannibalization concerns. (Customer) How do the needs of our current clients and new potential clients segments align? Can you create a product or service that meets their overlapping needs? (Complementary) What products or services can we create that would enhance our current products or services, or help our customers use more of our current products or services? (Christensen) Which new products or services could wipe out our current products or service? Can we buy, build, or partner to create it?

2. Draft an "elevator pitch"-style value proposition for a new product or service idea.

The Productize Pathway

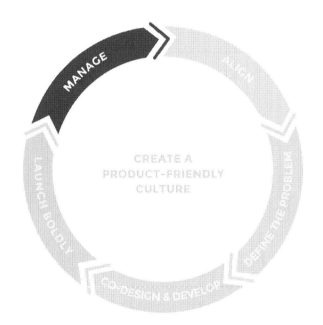

MANAGE

ALIGN

DEFINE THE PROBLEM

CO-DESIGN & DEVELOP

LAUNCH BOLDLY

CREATE A
PRODUCT-FRIENDLY
CULTURE

Chapter Eight

MISTAKE: Stopping at the MVP
SOLUTION: Manage and Iterate

Once your product is in the market, you move into the **Manage and Iterate** phase. During this phase, you measure and monitor the market's response to the product so that you can continue to iterate as you learn more. In this phase, I'll focus on four areas to help manage products:

- Developing a customer onboarding, customer success, and measurement strategy

- Monitoring and understanding the root causes of product performance

- Regular product performance reviews and roadmap updates

- Regular discussion on how the overall portfolio of products is performing

Basic questions to answer during this phase are: 1) Did we make something useful? 2) What are the best and worst parts of our product? 3) What shall we improve next?

While this is the last stage of the Productize Pathway, it's not the end of product innovation. Remember that product innovation is an iterative process that runs in a loop; it's not linear.

Developing a Customer Onboarding, Customer Success, and Measurement Strategy

A strong sales strategy for your new product is not enough. You also need a well-designed customer onboarding and success strategy.

A good onboarding and customer success process will achieve the following:

- Identify the key value drivers/product features that will ensure a great customer experience
- Develop and illustrate a clear implementation and use process
- Deliver early value

The benefits of designing a customer onboarding and success process are:

- Maximize renewals and upsell opportunities
- Improve buyer and user experience through an easy step-by-step process
- Boost customer loyalty
- Provide important product feedback for future development

Customer onboarding typically includes three phases:

1. Orientation and product training
2. Ongoing product usage monitoring and usage stimulation

3. Appropriate touchpoints to renew or upsell the product

A sample customer onboarding and success process for a larger-ticket enterprise product might look something like this:

- **Pre-sales support** to support sales team members, build relationships with buyers, and hand off the relationship from sales to customer success.

- **Buyer kick-off** in the first week to understand goals, organizational structure, and to set expectations and gain approval for the customer success plan which will support implementation and engagement.

- **User kick-off** and training in the first month with direct support, guides, training videos, etc.

- **Quarterly check-in with the buyer**. Check-ins include discussing product updates, asking for recommendations on activity and engagement, recruiting new users, gathering recommendations for upselling, and building the case for renewal. Consider monthly check-ins for customers who fall below target usage levels.

- **Engagement with users** as needed, using marketing support, such as:
  - o Immediate access to a demo video and welcome email
  - o Optional welcome video call within the first two weeks
  - o Monthly email check-in

A good process will not only outline the steps for onboarding and customer success, but the process will also provide the ideal time frame for each activity and the ideal level of product usage.

Since product use is a leading indicator that a customer will continue to buy and/or promote the product, defining the ideal level of usage serves as an early indicator of customer success. While you may track several key usage metrics, many companies find it useful to home in on "One Metric that Matters" (OMTM). The OMTM concept comes from Ben Yoskovitz's book, *Lean Analytics*, and it's the idea that even when tracking multiple metrics, there's one metric that we care about above all else. For example, one company included a live event as part of their product bundle and found that if a client attended the live event within the first 3 months of purchase, they were more likely to renew; therefore, live event attendance in the first 3 months was a good OMTM. A classic example of an OMTM is Facebook's "7 friends in 10 days" metric. A new user who connects with seven friends within the first ten days of joining is much more likely to become an active, lifetime user.

Understanding the Drivers Behind Product Performance

Not only does customer usage data serve as a leading indicator as to whether a customer is likely to continue to buy or not, but it also tells us *why.* To understand why a product is performing well (or not so well), we need to create a plan to test our original hypotheses about the product and not just look at the performance of certain product features. For example, why does the customer use the product? How do they use it? What sorts of benefits do they receive from it, etc.? Original product hypotheses (along with ease of use and overall customer satisfaction) should be regularly evaluated.

In order to track learning and document untested hypotheses, return to the hypothesis tracker introduced in Chapter Five. Ask questions such as:

- Are expectations clearly set during the sales process? Are we over-promising?

- Do customers have a clear sense of the product usage lifecycle?

- What do we need to know about our customers to provide them with a great experience during the onboarding process?

- How can we provide early value for the customer by focusing on their "job to be done"?

- What do customers need to do (and in what time frame) to get value from our product?

- What are early warning indicators that a customer may not continue or renew?

- What actions must our customers take regularly to drive growth and revenue (e.g., should we encourage cross-sell/upsell)?

- Are there other non-obvious points of customer interaction that could strengthen or erode value (e.g., marketing communications, billing)?

To answer these questions, use a mix of quantitative analysis (e.g., product usage data, customer data, etc.) and qualitative research, such as win/loss analysis to evaluate how many sales opportunities are won or lost and why; in addition, twice a year customer surveys, or advisory board feedback (as discussed previously) are also recommended using the research strategies and tactics discussed in Chapter Five. Analyzing product usage data by customer segments is very important, which is why data analysis is a valuable skill in any Product Manager's toolbox.

In addition to having an ongoing method for analyzing data related to product use and customer voice, you'll also need to keep an eye on competitors, as changes in competitor offerings might influence customer behavior. Reserve a few hours each quarter to refresh the competitor analysis discussed in Chapter Five and specifically focus on tracking changes to:

- Competitor health, such as: changes in company size (revenue and employees), primary investors, new funding rounds, new patents, etc.

- Key product attributes from the customer perspective, such as price, quality, delivery, ease of use

- Marketing strategies, such as content channels and content quality

Conduct a Regular Product Performance Review and Roadmap Update Conversation

Early stage products or MVPs shouldn't be released without defining a vision for them. Product roadmaps visualize a "best guess" about long-term product interactions, one that needs updating frequently based on what is learned from the build, measure, learn loop. A good product roadmap should:

- Keep teams focused on the highest priority initiatives

- Be simple and easy to understand so that all stakeholders know what to expect

- Reflect stakeholder input (where appropriate)

- Remain flexible to reflect ongoing customer input

- Not be too onerous to create

- Have realistic, measurable goals

Scoring methods discussed previously can be used here to score potential product enhancements against different variables, such as technical feasibility and desirability (customer need). Using objective criteria to score future enhancement ideas helps to avoid cognitive biases such as recency bias (e.g., "I put an idea on a roadmap because the last customer I talked to mentioned this"). Ideally, we collect input from a variety of sources to score each feature—the sales team, the leadership team, customer success, and our developers. Enhancements that score high can be placed on the roadmap, but enhancements that score low can go into the product backlog. (A product backlog is a list of the new features, changes to existing features, bug fixes, etc. that we may want to incorporate in the future.)

I suggest mapping out by quarter (i.e., outlining the plans for Q1, Q2, Q3, etc.) and building two versions of the roadmap. One version is internal and lists the new enhancements planned for each quarter, but also has product goals for each quarter (e.g., launch MVP, acquire five new customers) and the sales and marketing focus areas. The other version will be external-facing so that it can be shared with customers. The external version will be less detailed and have vague time horizons such as Now—Next—Later (NNL). An NNL roadmap divides the plan into three sections: what you're working on now, what you have planned next, and what you plan to work on later. A NNL roadmap is admittedly high-level, but it still shows customers and prospects how we plan to continuously improve the product.

Finally, as the product roadmap evolves, the business case must also evolve. Consider how your revenue and cost assumptions may be changing. What is your renewal rate? Average price point? Average lifetime customer value? Customer acquisition costs in addition to the costs of goods sold (COGS)? Ensure that the product is still meeting business objectives and that it will continue to do so in the future.

PRODUCT SWOT ANALYSIS INSTRUCTIONS

 PRODUCT FEATURE SCORING TEMPLATE

 PRODUCT ROADMAP TEMPLATES

(visit *www.theproductizebook.com* to download the tools.)

A Regular Review of How the Overall Portfolio of Products is Performing

Finally, it is important to establish a regular cadence of reviewing the progress of new product ideas and reallocating resources based on new information. If you have created a Product Innovation Board, this should be a key focus of the time they spend together.

It is easier to track progress if each product in the portfolio has a clearly articulated vision and performance measures. Just as I recommended creating a one-page strategy summary for each product idea when deciding on where to invest, I also recommend one for each product in the portfolio that includes answers to the following questions:

- **Vision:** What is our purpose for creating the solution? Which positive change should it bring about?

- **Target Group**: Which market or market segment does the solution address? Who are the target customers and users?

- **Customer Needs:** What meaningful, validated, urgent, and expensive problem does the solution solve? What benefits does it provide?

- **Solution:** What is the solution? What makes it stand out?

- **Business Goals:** What are the business goals?

The performance measures should mirror the criteria used in the Align phase to make product investment decisions (see Chapter Four). If, for example, a simple method of looking at revenue, confidence, and effort to prioritize ideas was used, reporting would show how revenue, confidence, and effort estimates have changed since the last meeting.

There are many benefits to regularly reviewing your portfolio of products and evaluating the entire health of the portfolio. These benefits include:

- Creating a cohesive strategy among products and services. How do products leverage the company's core strengths and assets? How are cross-sales supported?

- Deciding which products to grow, maintain, or harvest

- Creating a *regularly updated*, company-wide product and solutions roadmap that can be shared with customers

- Spotting opportunities to serve target markets with multiple products or services

- Making technology architecture decisions to support future growth and flexible solutions design

- Creating a robust pipeline of future ideas

 **PRODUCT PORTFOLIO ROADMAP TEMPLATE**

Action Steps

1. Hypothesize the "One Metric that Matters" for a new product or service that you have recently launched or are considering. What's the one signal that reveals that you are headed in the right direction?

2. Create a Now-Next-Later roadmap for your current and potential products and services portfolio. Keep it simple and limit it to one page.

CLOSING THOUGHTS

My hope is that after reading this book, you have the confidence you need and the tools you require to successfully guide your organization to innovate more scalable products and tech-enabled services. The processes I've outlined, the stories I've shared, and the tools on the website *www.productizebook.com* should provide the basics to get you started. As I mentioned at the beginning, you do not need to attempt all parts of the productization model at one time. You might recall that Empower started their journey to innovating more scalable products five years before hiring their first Chief Product Officer.

Also, don't be afraid to ask for help. I started Vecteris (www.vecteris.com) with a group of women with extensive experience designing and selling successful Information Services, SaaS and DaaS-based products. Our mission is to help companies build tech-enabled products and services to positively impact the world we live in. Our collaborative approach allows us to create lasting partnerships with our clients. We're here if you need the support. Our website is designed to be a resource where we share our latest thoughts and learnings, our Product Leader Peer Groups are a safe space for leaders to share their challenges and experiences, and for companies that need dramatic and meaningful change, we offer custom engagements and training.

At the very least, just keep in mind the three product innovation principles:

- Think Big, Start Small
- Follow Urgent, Expensive Customer Problems
- Be Fearless

Where you are or wherever you are going on your productization journey, keeping these principles in mind will help increase your success.

About the Author

Eisha Tierney Armstrong is the CEO and co-founder of Vecteris, where she works with companies ranging from start-ups to Fortune 500 companies on product innovation and product portfolio management. She has 25+ years of experience launching new data and information service products. Prior to co-founding Vecteris, Eisha held senior product leadership positions both with E.W. Scripps, the diversified media company, and with CEB (now Gartner), the world's largest membership-based corporate performance research and advisory company. Eisha earned her MBA at the Harvard Business School and her Bachelor of Arts in both Women's Studies and Economics at the University of Kansas.

3 STEPS TO GET STARTED NOW
to productize and scale your business

1. Download 25 Productization Pathway tools.
2. Complete the Product Innovation Maturity Diagnostic to assess your organization's productization readiness.
3. Get free access to The Productize Pathway™ Nano Series by author, Eisha Armstrong.

Go to **www.theproductizebook.com**

Competitive Analysis Template

Go-to-Market Checklist

Sample Interview Guide

Product Roadmap Template

"Vecteris helped us prepare for a global product launch in ways that we hadn't done before. They helped us create a playbook that not only helped us with this product launch, but also armed my team with a new way of thinking for future product launches."

- Global Head of Product

Let us help you avoid the most common productization mistakes.
Email us at **productize@vecteris.com** for a free consultation.

Spark
Productization Pathway Bootcamp

Spark's interactive workshops use a learn-by-doing approach to teach your team how to implement the Productize Pathway approach.

Evaluate and prioritize new product ideas

Align on the strategy and success criteria

Design and test a new product concept

Develop the business case

Learn more →
about Spark

Innovate with confidence. Act with speed.

❯ **Product Leader Peer Groups**
- Gain insight and validation
- Prepare for future challenges
- Build your network
- Navigate career obstacles
- Generate ideas to develop your team

❯ **Membership Perks:**
- Peer Leader Community
- Productization Coach
- Live Discussion
- Unlimited Access to Vecteris Library

Join →
Now